WALKING ROMAN ROADS IN THE FYLDE AND THE RIBBLE VALLEY

Walking Roman Roads in the Fylde and the Ribble Valley

by Philip Graystone S. M.

with introductory essays
by David Shotter and Katharine Buxton

Centre for North-West Regional Studies
University of Lancaster
1996

General Editor, Oliver M. Westall

Walking Roman Roads in the Fylde and the Ribble Valley
by Philip Graystone,
with introductory essays by David Shotter and Katharine Buxton

This volume is the thirty-first in a series published by the Centre for North-West Regional Studies at the University of Lancaster. Details of other titles in the series which are available may be found at the back of this volume.

ISSN 0308–4310

Published by the Centre for North-West Regional Studies,
University of Lancaster, 1996

Copyright © University of Lancaster, 1996
Text copyright © Philip Graystone,
David Shotter and Katharine Buxton, 1996

Typeset in Linotype Stempel Garamond by Carnegie Publishing Ltd,
18 Maynard St, Preston, Lancs.
Printed and bound in the UK by Redwood Books, Trowbridge

British Library Cataloguing in Publication Data
A CIP record for this book is available from the British Library

ISBN 0–901800–92–9

All rights reserved
No part of this publication may be reproduced, stored in a retrieval system, or transmitted in any form or by any means mechanical, electronic, photocopying or otherwise, without the prior permission of the publisher.

Contents

	Abbreviations	vi
	Preface	vii
	Roman Lancaster *by David Shotter*	1
	Roman Ribchester *by Katharine Buxton*	11
Part 1	Roman Roads in the Fylde and in the Ribble Valley: a general survey	21
Part 2	The Roman Road from Ribchester to Lancaster	23
Part 3	The Roman Road from Preston to Lancaster	45
Part 4	The Roman Road from Ribchester to Kirkham (and beyond)	61
Part 5	The Roman road leading eastwards from Ribchester along the Ribble Valley	69
Appendix	Finds of Roman material on or near the routes followed in this volume	83
	Bibliography	85

Abbreviations

BAR   *British Archaeological Reports*
CIL   *Corpus Inscriptionum Latinarum*
CW²   *Transactions of the Cumberland and Westmorland Antiquarian and Archaeological Society* (Second Series).
ILS   *Inscriptiones Latinae Selectae*
RIB   *Roman Inscriptions of Britain*

Preface

This is the third volume in the series about Roman roads in north-west England. Like the previous two, it attempts to combine archaeological accuracy with general interest, and is intended primarily for the enthusiast who wishes to explore in the field – preferably on foot – the remains of these roads.

Once again I must thank Dr David Shotter for providing a scholarly historical introduction – this time on Roman Lancaster – a key point in the Fylde road network and one about which he can claim expert knowledge. I must also acknowledge his kind permission to reproduce, on page 42, the milestone inscriptions and the photograph of the statuary from Burrow Heights. A valuable contribution to this volume is the second introductory essay from the pen of Katharine Buxton of the Lancaster University Archaeological Unit. Her subject is the other focal point in the network, the fort of Ribchester, where she was one of the directors of the recent excavation. I am grateful also for the help and encouragement given me by various correspondents, especially Dr D. J. Woolliscroft, Alan Richardson and T. M. Allan. Particularly helpful in the preparation of this volume has been the information supplied by Gordon Heald.

As in my previous volumes, I must acknowledge my indebtedness to the late Ivan D. Margary, whose *Roman Roads in Britain* is the standard work on the subject and is likely to remain so. I have also found very useful the previous survey, with the same title, by Thomas Codrington. Other documentary sources consist mainly of notes and papers scattered throughout the transactions of historical and archaeological societies; these are acknowledged, usually in abbreviated form, whenever they are used in the text, and a full list is given in the bibliography at the end of the volume. Many readers, hopefully, will be more interested in field exploration than in library research, but I trust that they will not find the references irksome; after all, it is useful to know where to look if you wish to follow up some particular detail that has caught your interest. (Dr Shotter and Katharine Buxton, of course, list separate bibliographies for their introductory essays).

The sketch maps accompanying the text are not, as is evident, meant for use in the field. They are merely rough indications of road routes and of the location of various features and (sometimes) of photographs. As guides in field investigation, the appropriate

Ordnance Survey maps are indispensable, especially the invaluable Pathfinder series. For this volume the Pathfinder maps required are : Nos. 648, 659, 668, 669, 678, 679, 680, and 688. If this is considered too expensive an outlay, the O.S. Landranger series nos. 97, 102, and 103 will cover the area, though far less effectively.

In the actual exploratory work which preceded this volume, I must acknowledge the help given me by my brother Frank on several occasions. Mrs Trudie Slater very helpfully pointed out to me traces of the Ribchester/Kirkham road in the area east of Tun Brook, and Mrs Mason kindly invited me to investigate the fields around Puddle House Farm, Poulton le Fylde. Assistance at a much earlier date was provided by Mr E. Holgate of Standen Hey Farm, near Clitheroe, who in the 1950s allowed me, with the help of my pupils, to excavate two sections on the fascinating Roman road which traverses his land. The results are described in the appropriate chapter.

Philip Graystone

Roman Lancaster

David Shotter

DESPITE the imposing nature of the Castle and the Priory Church, Lancaster's development in medieval times was relatively slow; Scottish attacks and epidemics ensured that it remained a modest town until the eighteenth century, when the development of the port and its trading across the Atlantic led to a new prosperity, which was amongst other things translated into building. The fact that Lancaster has little to show for the medieval period and that its oldest buildings are predominantly Georgian is a consequence of this 'arrested development'.[1]

Many of the major finds of Roman material in Lancaster came to light during the period of expansion in the eighteenth century and later in the following century when major services, such as sewers and railways, were under construction. Nonetheless, references to ancient structures and Roman finds go back well beyond that; Leland, Camden and many others[2] reported walls on Castle Hill and in the area of Church Street, but these reports were dominated by speculation on the significance of the Wery Wall – speculation which persisted until the questions about it were finally resolved in the excavations of 1973. The Wery Wall – the name means no more than 'Old' Wall – has dominated the thinking of historians and archaeologists, although it represents only a small part (albeit of importance) of Lancaster's Roman history.

Historians of Lancaster are fortunate in that the record of much that was found was ably kept by such men as Father Thomas West (in his *Guide to the Lakes*, published in 1778) and Edward Baines (in his *History of the County Palatine of Lancaster*, published in 1824); further, lists of material which had been found were collated and published by W. Thompson Watkin (in his *Roman Lancaster* of 1883). These, and other less well-known antiquarians ensured that a great deal of what was uncovered was not lost, and published their observations made at times when the townscape presented an appearance very different from that which exists today.[3] A more detailed, but no less significant example of this kind of service is provided by the recording by Thomas Dalzell and Corbyn Barrow of Roman coins found in the nineteenth century. Their notebooks, meticulously kept, are preserved in Lancaster Museum, and have enabled provenances to be attached to many coins in the Museum's collection. Some of the sites reported by such writers as these have been 'tested' by intermittent excavations, conducted on a wide variety of scales in the present century.[4]

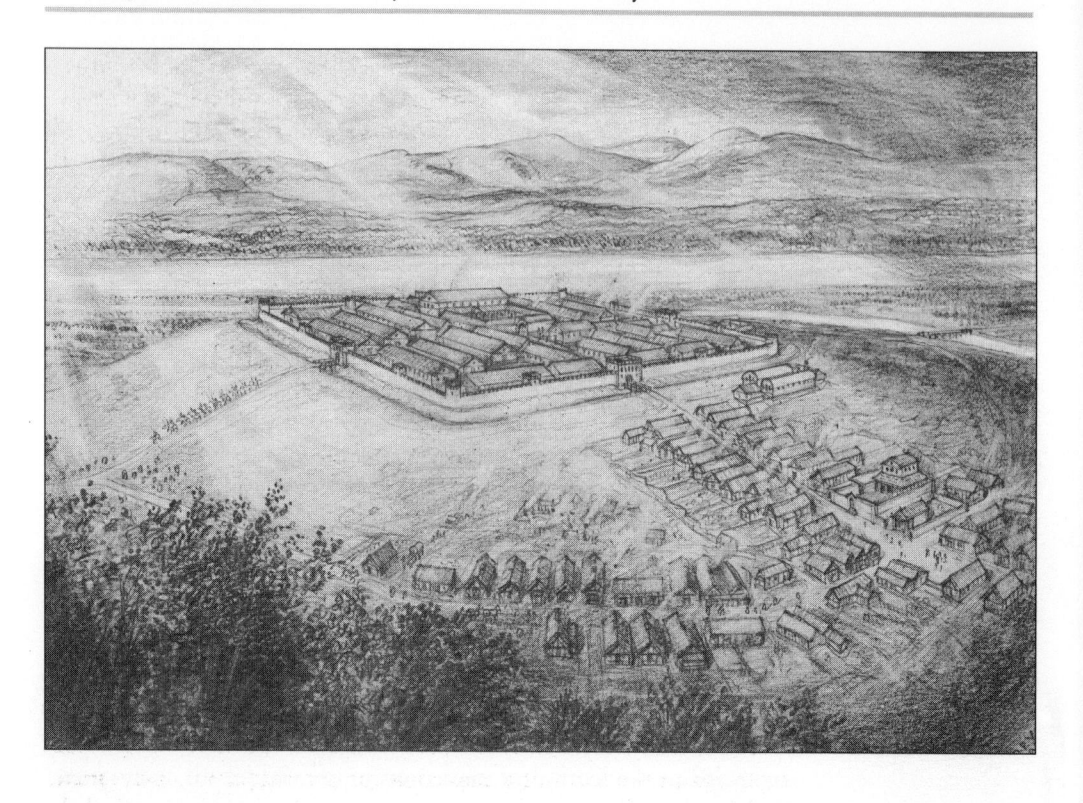

As a consequence, we are often able to put antiquarian reports alongside the results of excavations, and arrive at plausible accounts of aspects and parts at least of Lancaster's history as a Roman fort and civilian settlement (*vicus*). Of course, there are still many gaps, both physical and chronological, in our understanding, and the non-availability to excavation of crucial areas, such as are covered by the Castle and the Priory Church, is likely to leave a number of our questions unanswered for a considerable time to come.

It has long been assumed that the earliest, permanent, occupation of the fort-site on Castle Hill occurred during the governorship of Agricola, presumably during the course of his second campaign (AD 78). Tacitus' reference in his account of that campaign of the Roman army's occupation in an area of 'estuaries and woods' seems appropriate to Lancaster and its hinterland.[5] Roman forts of Agricola's time were generally square or rectangular, with ramparts of clay or clay-and-turf. The external face of the rampart would have been battered and the inside often revetted with vertical timbers. Outside there would have been one or more 'V'-shaped ditches, and perhaps

A reconstruction by David Vale of the Roman fort and civil settlement of Lancaster in the second century AD, as it might have appeared from high ground to the south-east. (Reproduced by kind permission of David Vale, from D. Shotter and A. White, *The Romans in Lunesdale*, CNWRS, Lancaster, 1995).

timber palisades also, whilst inside a metalled service-road (the *intervallum*-road) ran all the way round the fort's perimeter. The buildings would have been constructed of timber, and the ramparts pierced with at least four timber gate-and-guardtower complexes.[6] Elements of such structures have been identified in at least four excavations on Castle Hill, including a very fine rampart-section adjacent to the Old Vicarage; the excavations have in fact located elements of the defences on all sides of the hill, with the exception of the south. Further, these defences appear to have had two phases of activity followed by a period (probably short) of abandonment. It has been assumed that the second phase, which represented an enlargement of the first fort, was constructed in the 80s AD, perhaps following the general withdrawal from northern Scotland in *c.*AD 86–7.

It is, however, worth considering alternative models: the presence in the recorded coin-sample of pre-Flavian *aes* (copper/bronze) coins is suggestive of the possibility of activity at Lancaster prior to Agricola's governorship; indeed, within that group of coins the fact that a number are earlier than Nero's reign may point to military operations at this point of the Lancashire coast as early as the 60s AD. A context for such activity is provided by the deteriorating stability of Brigantian politics at the time.[7] If the Lancaster area was included at so early a date, the likely *structural* evidence for it would be found in the form of a campaign-camp rather than a permanent fort. In view of the fact that it is now regarded as certain that Carlisle and Ribchester were established as permanent forts during the governorship of Petilius Cerialis (AD 71–4), it is not inconceivable that the two Flavian phases recognised at Lancaster belong to Cerialis and Agricola, and are followed by a period of abandonment from the late 80s into the middle or late 90s.

The northern rampart of the primary fort was 9 feet wide, and, despite great vertical compression, still stood to a height of 5 feet with a very clearly battered outer face; it was constructed of clay-and-turf, on a brushwood-foundation. Elsewhere, evidence was found of a timber guard-tower at the north-east corner, and elements of the eastern gateway, so positioned as to indicate the Roman origin of Church Street. Outside this eastern gate, there were two ditches with evidence of a palisade of timber stakes on the inner lip of the second ditch; these ditches appeared to be curving inwards through 90 degrees, as if to accommodate the fort's exit-road. The only evidence of internal buildings was of two phases of timber-structures (probably barracks) near to the Old Vicarage; these had evidently been destroyed by fire.

The dimensions of this fort would appear to have been approximately 615 feet (east to west) by approximately 400 feet (north to south), although the latter dimension must remain conjectural since the southern side of the fort has never been revealed and presumably lies beneath the Castle. Such dimensions would argue for a fort with an area of approximately 5.6 acres, which puts it on the larger side, but comparable with Ribchester.

The second Flavian phase involved enlargement by pushing the northern rampart northwards by about 120 feet; if this was matched on the southern side, the fort's eastern and western ramparts would have extended to around 650 feet in length, producing a fort which, at over 9 acres, was large for the period. Further, the general shape will thereby have been changed from rectangular to nearly square. If, in the primary phase, the main gateway lay on the eastern side, it is possible that in the secondary phase the fort was reoriented through 90 degrees, moving the main gateway to the north, although this *may* have happened later.

We have evidence at various periods of cavalry-units being based at Lancaster; the *ala Augusta* and the *ala Sebosiana* are cited on inscriptions,[8] and near the east gateway a timber-lined well had been filled with stable-refuse. Certainly, the primary phase of the fort was sufficiently large to house a 500-strong cavalry-unit, whilst the enlarged fort may have been garrisoned by a 1,000-strong cavalry-unit, or by a smaller unit in association with a detachment, perhaps of legionary troops. At any rate, the size of the fort is a clear indication of its significance in the policing network established in north-west England.

Early in the second century,[9] after reoccupation, the fort was further refurbished – on this occasion by adding a stone-wall to the face of the secondary clay-and-turf rampart, and probably by replacing some at least of the internal buildings in stone. It is probably significant that some of the timbers which were recovered from the timber-lined well situated near the east gate of the fort represented re-used building material. Little is known of this fort, although the medieval rampart-system visible in the western Vicarage field is known to overlie precisely the north-west corner of the defences of the Trajanic fort.

Coin-evidence suggests that the fort may have lost at least part of its garrison with the renewed push into Scotland ordered by Antoninus Pius in AD 142. Although the Antonine Wall was abandoned by the mid-160s and troops presumably returned to Hadrian's Wall and northern England, it is unclear what happened at Lancaster: structural and artefactual evidence do not present a coherent picture. However, in view of the fact that the *vicus* continued to thrive through the later second century, it might be suggested that, after the Antonine occupation of Scotland, the large fort at Lancaster did not receive back a *full* garrison; occupation by a unit of *normal* size – that is, 500 men – might be expected to have left areas of the fort apparently unoccupied. It will not be possible to resolve such dilemmas until more is known of the southern end of the fort, and an opportunity arises to study a substantial area of the fort's interior. A further point of consideration is that the large courtyard-building, parts of which have been excavated in the northern Vicarage field, would appear to have obtruded upon the northern defences of the fort.

In the middle of the third century AD we have clear evidence of occupation in the form of an inscription[10] commemorating the rebuilding from ground-level of a bath-house and basilica which had 'collapsed through old age'. The bath-house is almost certainly that which stood immediately outside the eastern rampart of the fort, whilst the basilica is best understood as a *basilica equestris exercitatoria*, a special drill-hall attached to the headquarters-buildings of cavalry-forts. If these important buildings had in fact collapsed through old age, this might suggest that the rebuilding followed a period of neglect, presumably because of demilitarisation. On the other hand, such a formula might represent a euphemism to cover violent destruction. At any rate, reconstruction was carried out by the *ala Sebosiana*, a cavalry-unit, whose name figures on a lead-sealing from the western Vicarage field, and also on a lead-sealing found at Brough-under-Stainmore and on a writing-tablet from Carlisle.[11]

It has already been suggested that Lancaster's size argues for the fort a considerable local (or regional) importance, and that its garrison may at one time have been partly legionary; this suggestion receives some support from the fact that the collection of stamped roofing-tiles[12] from Lancaster itself and its associated tilery at Quernmore includes one fragment from Lancaster with a possible legionary origin. Further, a dedication survives which was made to the Romano-Celtic god, Mars Cocidius, by a high-ranking official, Lucius Vibenius, who is described as the governor's aide (*beneficiarius consularis*).[13] It is possible that the large courtyard-building identified in the northern Vicarage field was his official residence.

Major changes were made to the fort in the fourth century; around AD 330, a completely new fort was constructed, of which the Wery Wall was a part. This fort was built on a new alignment and destroyed buildings which stood in its way, such as the bath-house of the courtyard building. As stated above, the Wery Wall itself appears to represent the core of an external bastion (or artillery-mounting) which stood at the north angle of this fort. Other possible elements of this fort have been located over the years, which suggest a structure which was sub-rectangular, enclosing an area in excess of 5.5 acres, and possibly as large as 9 acres. The fact that this structure was characterised by thick, heavy – and presumably, high – stone walls suggests a parallel with sites on the west coast such as Cardiff, Caernarfon and Caer Gybi, and with the series of 'Saxon-Shore' forts in the south-east.

This apparent attention to coastal defence fits well with the changing military imperatives of Roman Britain in the fourth century; it should also be noted that the discovery on Cockersands Moss of two statuettes to the Celtic sea-god, Nodens (or Nodons), strengthens Lancaster's maritime connections in the fourth century;[14] for a new temple to this god was constructed at Lydney, on the Severn estuary, *after* AD 360, and contains a mosaic which possibly carries the title of the commander of what survived of the British fleet (*classis Britannica*). The Lancaster-area has also produced an inscription[15] which contains the name of a unit with clear maritime connections – a unit of bargemen (*numerus barcariorum*). Such soldiers may have, amongst other things, acted as lightermen, unloading deep-draughted vessels in Morecambe Bay, and bringing their cargoes into port at Lancaster. This inscription, which was found at Halton-on-Lune, is not specifically dated, but may indicate a unit in garrison at the new fort at Lancaster in the fourth century with skills suitable to a coastal site and which equipped it to handle the type of threat which was emerging in the fourth century.

No internal buildings of this new fort have been recognised, and it is possible that it housed both soldiers and civilians, since recent excavations in the *vicus* have indicated an abandonment of properties there around AD 340, presumably as the security-situation in the north-west became more tenuous. Certainly, disruption was caused in the 340s and 350s by the feuding between the sons of Constantine and the emergence in the west of the rebel-emperor, Magnentius. This was followed shortly afterwards by the so-called 'conspiracy of the barbarians' in AD 367 which inflicted much damage to military sites in the north, but which was followed by reconstruction which appears to have enhanced the importance of coastal sites such as Ravenglass, Maryport and Bowness-on-Solway. That occupation of the Wery-Wall fort continued late in the fourth and probably into the fifth centuries is clear from the evidence both of pottery and coins. In common with other sites in the north, it is likely that, by the early fifth century, the occupants of the fort exercised a purely local function of supplying and defending themselves, and might be best described as a local militia.

Most Roman forts supported extra-mural civilian settlement, since the presence of a garrison of well-paid troops represented a market which had needs which others could supply for profit. In the case of Lancaster, the vibrancy of such a settlement will have been enormously enhanced by the additional role of a port. Although there may have been extra-mural settlement all around the fort, it is likely to have been most concentrated to the east and north-east of the fort, between Church Street and the river. Although no reports of harbour-facilities by the riverside have ever been confirmed, it seems inconceivable that they did not exist.

It is likely that the civilian-settlements enjoyed different levels of status, and certainly grew to different sizes, depending presumably on their commercial success. It is, however, becoming increasingly clear that it is dangerous to generalise about them, although this inevitably happens since so few have been substantially investigated.[16]

Excavations and aerial photography appear to indicate that such settlements were not planned, but grew in an informal way as need and opportunity dictated. It is likely that, since they fell under the general jurisdiction of the fort-commander, most did not have a civilian administration and therefore lacked the buildings that went with such a role. Buildings usually in evidence are a bath-house, a hotel (*mansio*), temples to accommodate a wide variety of official and unofficial religious cults, bars and brothels. The most common structures, however, were the long, narrow, strip-buildings, situated with their gable-ends fronting the streets; some of these might have provided living-accommodation for soldiers' families, whilst others might be better described as business-premises, consisting of a shop on the street-frontage, with living-accommodation behind it, and perhaps, at the rear, a yard where the owners/tenants could make or process what was sold in the shop. It is possible by analogy with other sites that areas of these settlements were devoted to particular activities. We might expect that many would be involved in the food-trade, or in manufacturing objects in cloth, leather, terra-cotta, or metal.

In the case of Lancaster, existing evidence suggests that the settlement centred on present-day Church Street, the exit-road from the fort's east gate. However, there is also evidence of settlement on the north and west flanks of the fort. Evidently, the most significant building so far located is situated on Castle Hill itself immediately outside the postulated position of the fort's north gate. It appears to have been a large courtyard-building with a bath-suite at the southern end. The hey-day of this building seems to have been in the later second and third centuries and it was destroyed by the construction of the Wery Wall fort in or around AD 330.[17] It was evidently a building of some consequence, not only because it had its own bath-suite, but also because of the amount of painted wall-plaster found amongst its debris.[18] Although its overall dimensions are difficult to recover, it appears to have occupied a space of approximately 180 feet by 80 feet. The obvious interpretations of this building are *either* that it was a *mansio* (hotel for official travellers) *or* that it was the residence of an important official, such as a regional centurion (*centurio regionarius*) or a governor's aide (*beneficiarius consularis*).[19]

The fort's bath-house was located just outside the eastern rampart, and is now encased in concrete beneath the office-block known as Mitre House. The bath-house was studied under very unfavourable conditions in 1973–4, and any conclusions are tentative; however, one area produced a substantial hypocaust, constructed probably in the second century. The floor-supports were provided by *pilae* of square tiles, although these had been supplemented by roughly-hewn stone *pilae*, presumably to halt sagging to the floor. It is not impossible that these represent the repairs alluded to in the third-century bath-house inscription.[20] A further building contained architectural debris of a type that suggested that it might have been of the *basilica*-type.

Other buildings in the civilian settlement have been recorded or viewed at various times in fragmentary form along Church Street, China Street, Cheapside and Penny Street,[21] although considerable damage has been done to archaeological deposits on street-frontages by cellar-digging. Little substantial information has emerged to indicate the purposes of buildings, although most appear to have been of the strip-building type, constructed in timber or stone-and-timber and separated by 'ditches' or alley-ways ('lanes'), some of which still run between Church Street and Market Street. There is an indication of a possible temple-site on the southern side of Church Street, and adjacent to a site excavated in 1988 and 1992, which itself produced fragments of a pottery-mask, possibly of Dionysiac type. Although buildings tested have individual chronologies, an overall date for the civilian settlement appears to run from the late first century AD to the mid-fourth.

It is possible, too, that there was a temple of the Persian god, Mithras, somewhere near to the fort; such temples were not uncommon in the second and third centuries AD. The evidence in the case of Lancaster consists of a group of statuary, which was found in 1794 to the south of Lancaster during canal-digging,[22] and evidently not in its original location. One of the heads appears to have the 'Phrygian cap' familiar in Mithraic sculpture. However, an alternative explanation has been put forward that the statues represent a group from a large mausoleum, which is a possible interpretation of an earth-work at Burrough Heights (about two miles south of the fort), which lies close to the road running south from Lancaster to Walton-le-Dale.[23]

Roman law forbade the burial of the dead *within* settlements, and so, according to custom, burials were placed by the sides of roads leading out of settlements; evidence of cremations has come from the southern end of Penny Street, and of inhumations from West Road. The discovery in Cheapside of a tombstone of a cavalry-soldier, Lucius Julius Apollinaris, may indicate the location nearby of the eastern cemetery, although the stone had itself evidently been re-used for building purposes.

Whilst, therefore, a picture emerges with some detail of an important fort with a thriving civilian settlement, a great deal more work is required to fill in further important detail, and to expand and confirm what are initial impressions. As we shall see later, however, it can be assumed that the presence of a vigorous fort and town at Lancaster will have had implications further afield. Local farmers will have been presented with an opportunity to supply this large market, as well as being in part *required* to supply it through their taxes. Some land will probably have been confiscated and used by the cavalry-unit itself to grow fodder and bedding for its horses, whilst still more will have been appropriated for use as discharge-gratuities for retiring soldiers, such as Julius Januarius;[24] this soldier, who was settled about a mile to the north of the fort, displayed his integration into the society and economy of the lower Lune valley by making a dedication to Jalonus Contrebis, who was in all probability, the Romano-Celtic spirit of the river Lune, on whose continuing favour soldier and civilian alike depended.

Notes

1. For a full treatment of the discovery and interpretation of Roman Lancaster, see Shotter and White (1990). Excavations since 1950 are discussed in Jones and Shotter (1988), and also in Geoffrey Leather's privately published *Roman Lancaster: Some Excavation Reports and some Observations* (Preston, 1972).
2. For relevant passages, see Shotter and White (1990), pp. 6 and 33.
3. See Penney (1981).
4. The locations of these are given in Shotter and White (1990), pp. 11–12.
5. *Life of Agricola*, 20,2.
6. M. J. Jones (1975).
7. The evidence is discussed in Shotter (1994).
8. *RIB* 606 (*ala Augusta*); *RIB* 605 (*ala Sebosiana*). In general, see Shotter and White 1990), pp. 27–31.
9. *RIB* 604; dating to c.AD 102.
10. *RIB* 605; see Jones and Shotter (1988), pp. 208–11.
11. For the sealing from western Vicarage field, see Shotter and White 1990), p. 65; for that from Brough-under-Stainmore, see Richmond (1936), p. 120. The reference from Carlisle is *Tab. Luguv.* 19 (see I. D. Caruana, *The Roman Forts at Carlisle: Excavations at Annetwell Street, 1973–84* [forthcoming]). Other references to the unit may be found in the discharge-diploma found at Malpas in Cheshire (*CIL* XVI. 48), on a tombstone from Mainz on the Rhine (*ILS* 2533) and on a dedication from Co. Durham (*RIB* 1041) which records a successful boar-hunting expedition by the unit's commander.
12. Shotter and White (1990), pp. 64ff.
13. *RIB* 602.
14. *RIB* 616 and 617; both statuettes are now lost.
15. *RIB* 601; See Shotter (1973).
16. The sites from which generalisations are often made are Vindolanda (see R. Birley, 1977) and Manchester (see Jones, 1974).
17. Jones and Shotter (1988), pp. 61–71.
18. Jones and Shotter (1988), pp. 160–6.
19. *RIB* 602.
20. *RIB* 605; see Jones and Shotter (1988), pp. 72–6.
21. Shotter and White (1990), pp. 32–46.
22. Watkin (1883), pp. 180ff.
23. Edwards (1971).
24. *RIB* 600.

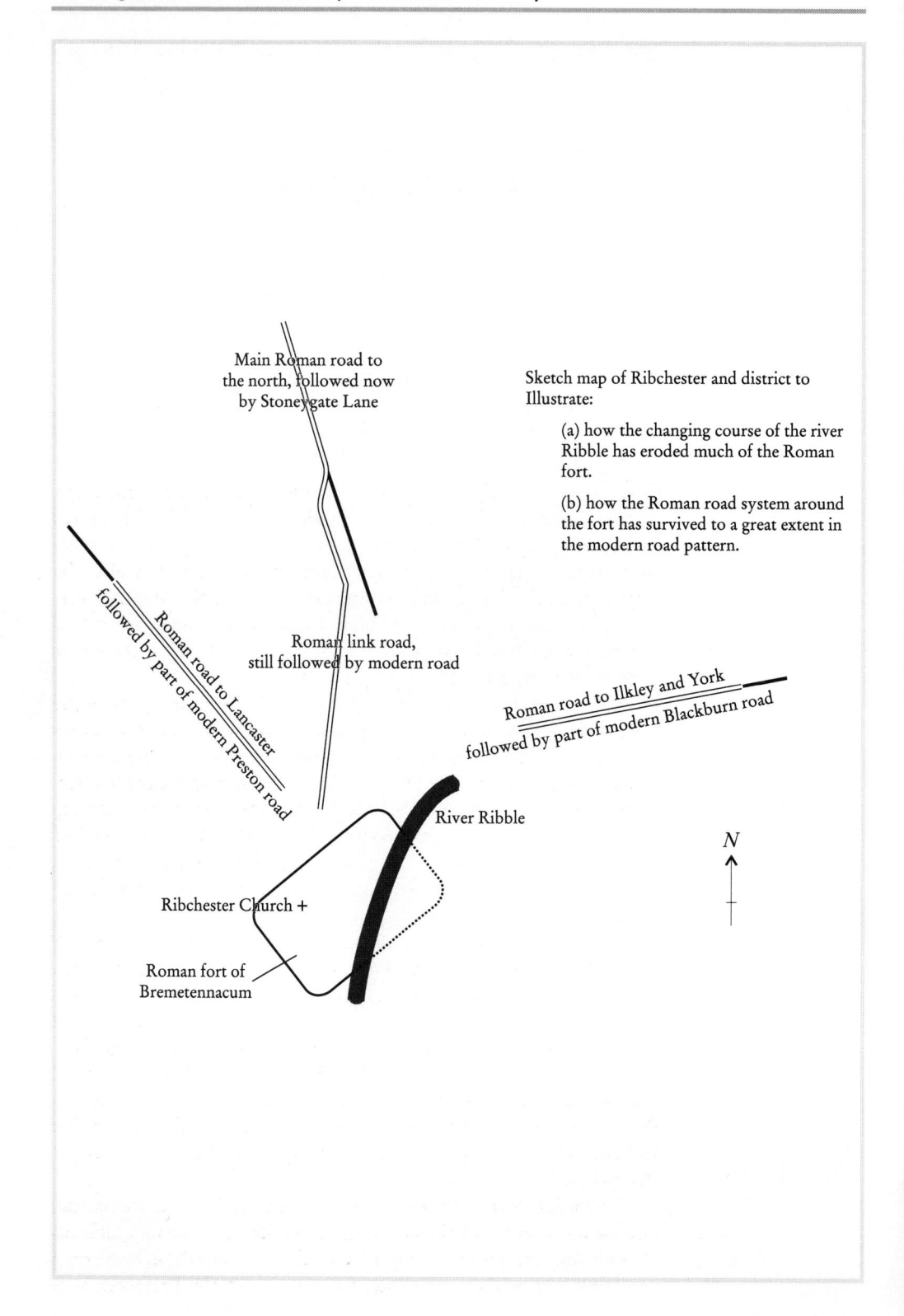

Walking Roman Roads in the Fylde and Ribble Valley

Main Roman road to the north, followed now by Stoneygate Lane

Sketch map of Ribchester and district to Illustrate:

(a) how the changing course of the river Ribble has eroded much of the Roman fort.

(b) how the Roman road system around the fort has survived to a great extent in the modern road pattern.

Roman road to Lancaster followed by part of modern Preston road

Roman link road, still followed by modern road

Roman road to Ilkley and York followed by part of modern Blackburn road

River Ribble

Ribchester Church +

Roman fort of Bremetennacum

N

Roman Ribchester

Katharine Buxton

It is written upon a wall in Rome,
Ribchester was as rich as any town in Christendom.

So goes the old rhyme, attributed to the inhabitants of Ribchester by the antiquarian William Camden, in 1586.[1] It still serves admirably, in a modern context, to describe not only the considerable range of structural remains found in the town, but also the wealth of less tangible information gleaned from this material evidence; information which tells us not simply of Roman activity in Ribchester itself, but also allows us to set the fort within the wider context of Roman military activity in the north-west.

Ribchester, in central Lancashire, lies on the northern bank of the River Ribble. The Roman fort, the south-eastern third of which has been swept away by the river, lies to the south-west of the modern village, largely beneath the graveyard and parish church of St Wilfrid. Contemporary extra-mural settlement has been observed, running for at least 500m northwards from the fort,[2] and evidence from other parts of the modern village indicates that the Roman settlement must have been extensive; perhaps rather more than conventionally assumed for an auxiliary fort, such as Ribchester.

Little is known of activity in the area before the Romans arrived, although there is little doubt that it was occupied from time to time. A circular ditch, discovered c.200m north of the church[3] enclosed five Bronze Age cremations, buried in Collared Urns; and Portfield Camp hill fort, which produced goldwork of late Bronze Age date, and was probably occupied during the early Iron Age, lies only a few kilometres up-river. Otherwise though, the Iron Age in Ribchester, as in the county as a whole, remains all but invisible archaeologically, a phenomenon much speculated upon, but as yet unexplained.

The earliest fort built at what was to become Bremetenacum, can now be dated with confidence to the early 70s AD, probably built AD 71–4 during the governorship of Cerialis.[4] Effectively erected on a greenfield site within the western territories of the Brigantes, it is likely that its foundation was driven exclusively by Roman tactical considerations, perhaps taking advantage of the break-up of the 'Brigantian Federation' to establish a foothold in the area. It became, however, one of the few forts in the region to remain in occupation throughout the Romano-British period, suggesting that it was of considerable importance to the economy, security, and management of this part of the Roman north. Its position, at an important intersection in the Roman communications system, and at a crossing point (ford or bridge?) of the River Ribble, must have been a major logistical asset. Roman Ribchester oversaw the crossroads of the important north–south route, from Chester to Carlisle, with one of the few good trans-Pennine routes, from Kirkham to York. It seems more than likely that, in the first and second centuries AD, both fort and extra-mural settlement were closely concerned in the rapid movement of troops and supplies throughout the region, and later, in the third century, auxiliary cavalry such as those stationed at Ribchester, seem to have acted more or less as rapid response teams, effectively policing the area.

The first fort was, typically, built of timber felled locally, mainly large oaks, several hundred years old. The fort buildings were surrounded by a turf-and-clay rampart raised on a substantial foundation, a wooden raft (corduroy) which helped prevent the heavy structure from literally sinking into the boggy ground by the riverside. It was further defended by a series of substantial V-shaped ditches dug around the periphery of the fort. It seems, however, that these defences were seldom needed in earnest, for during this period it appears that a significant number of horses may have been routinely stabled outside the fort, beyond the ditches.

Brigantia, a client state of Rome, latterly under the authority of Cartimandua and her consort Venutius, was at this time riven by internal strife. Rome had intervened in support of the Queen, presumably to maintain the *status quo*, and western Brigantia, probably the natural power-base of her estranged husband Venutius, appears to have been indifferent to the Roman presence at this time, although not actively hostile. The fort was probably built to accommodate a largely temporary garrison, and finds from recent excavations[5] suggest the earliest garrison might have been somewhat ostentatious, perhaps sent to indulge in an episode of 'flag-waving' to 'impress the natives'.[6] This rather flamboyant phase appears to have been short-lived, presumably as front-line troops moved on to continue their campaigns elsewhere. The fort does not, however, appear to have been completely abandoned. Stratigraphic and environmental evidence from the recent excavations suggest a much-reduced garrison, living under some considerable stress. The fort-buildings were allowed to fall into disrepair, and its defences filled with rubbish, much of it stable waste, apparently deliberately dumped into the flooded ditches. Animal-bone[7] and palaeoenvironmental studies[8] imply that food was, at times, scarce, suggesting both that supply was unpredictable, and that trade with the indigenous population was on a rather *ad hoc* basis, rather than with regular sources of supply.

Agricola's army appears to have refurbished the fort during his northern campaigns in the late 70s. The rampart was strengthened, the ditches recut, the ramshackle stabling in the extra-mural area demolished and reorganised, and, one presumes, the internal buildings either rebuilt or refurbished. It has been suggested, that during his push northwards Agricola used his troops and fleet *in tandem*,[9] using the ships to transport troops, who disembarked in the main estuaries and marched up the river-valleys to join with others, presumably the main army, taking overland routes. Excavation evidence[10] suggests that the early, Agricolan, occupation of Kirkham, down river to the west, comprised a series of marching camps, presumably short-lived accommodation for troops landing in the Ribble estuary, before marching inland to the central garrison/supply-base at Ribchester, whence they were dispatched northwards as and when they were needed. Indeed the fortunes of the two sites appear to have remained closely connected, their complementary roles persisting until at least the middle of the second century.

As the active frontier swept north, the fort at Ribchester would have been left to control the military hinterland between the settled and frontier zones, and although, once again, the majority of the garrison presumably moved northwards, the fort appears to have been successfully transformed from a frontline/frontier installation to a more settled, behind-the-lines stronghold. Although troop numbers in the garrison might have remained fairly small, evidence from excavation suggests that adequate and reliable sources of supply were soon established.

The practical lifetime of a turf-and-timber fort, before radical repair was needed, is estimated at 20 to 30 years,[11] and at least two Flavian phases of timber building have been identified within the Ribchester fort.[12] Presumably, by the end of the Trajanic period, the fort was again becoming fairly run down, although there is no evidence to suggest that it was ever abandoned. The fort and known extra-mural buildings were again demolished, or at least extensively refurbished around this time, probably between AD 117 and 125.[13] Although rebuilding in stone was common military practice in northern England during the early years of the second century, it can be speculated that the growing need for a secure, behind-the-lines, supply-and-distribution-centre to service the flurry of activity generated by the construction of Hadrian's Wall, may have been the immediately stimulus for the reconstruction of the fort in stone.

The interior of the fort was reorganised; excavation shows that the commander's house,[14] tentatively identified within the Flavian fort, was demolished and replaced by a series of barrack-blocks. The defences, too, were updated. The western part of the rampart was cut back for the insertion of a stone revetment, and much of the redundant corduroy and rampart material was thrown into the early ditches, which were subsequently cleaned or re-dug on a number of occasions.[15] On the northern side of the fort the rampart appears to have been completely destroyed, in order to make way for a deliberately planned industrial complex. The total removal of the original defences in this area appears to have necessitated the construction of a large, temporary ditch to mark and defend the limits of the construction area. With the completion of the new fort, the ditch became redundant, and was filled rapidly with a vast dump of organic rubbish. This material probably represented the debris from something of a 'spring clean', much of it apparently originating from a specialist workshop (probably a leather-worker), presumably demolished or renovated during this period.

There seems little doubt that extra-mural activity was at its most extensive during the second century, although the enhanced political status which might be expected to accompany this growth, is not epigraphically attested until the third.[16] Excavations to the north of the fort[17] suggest that there was a military controlled annex immediately beyond the defences which contained at least one large timber framed metalworking (?) workshop, whilst, further away, there were wooden strip-houses of the type often associated with civilian shops and workshops.[18] Although Ribchester does not appear to have been a major industrial centre, its primary function was perhaps to redistribute a range of goods accumulated from production-centres elsewhere, such as Walton-le-Dale and Wilderspool; however, the presence of these workshops with hearths, smithing waste,[19] and specialist tools,[20] certainly indicates that some manufacturing was taking place at the site.

It has always been accepted that Ribchester was a cavalry-fort, and both epigraphic and material evidence serve to underline this supposition. Asturian cavalry are known to have been stationed at the fort, probably in the second century,[21] while Sarmatian heavy cavalry were sent there in the third.[22] Not only were cavalry-fittings and horse-tack common in the copper alloy and leather assemblages of the most recent excavations,[23] but also copious quantities of stable waste and horse manure were detected by environmentalists studying soil samples from the site. Cavalry-units would undoubtedly require considerable backup to provide replacement-mounts, grazing, hay, and feed, which must have been drawn from a wide area. Evidence for large military structures has been found some considerable way north of the fort,[24] and although many interpretations can be suggested for the complex, one convincing explanation might be that the area was used for corrals and stabling. Perhaps Ribchester acted as a kind of livery and training depot.

In contrast to the south, where Roman conquest included the smooth assimilation and modification of existing social and economic traditions, the north presented a substantially less-developed context. It seems likely that extra-mural settlements at forts such as Ribchester were effectively plantations, remaining under military control for quite some time, in an attempt to foster a market-economy in an otherwise-undeveloped area. To this extent they were not simply the haphazard agglomeration of settlers and service-providers usually imagined hanging onto the purse strings of a fort, but were possibly purpose-built, and certainly actively encouraged, by the military establishment. They must have served not only to provide a venue for local contact and exchange, but also to manage and service an enormous, highly organised, and probably fragile, supply-network for the army. This requirement may well have been the underlying stimulus for the creation of the extra-mural complex at Ribchester, and without doubt, the later, more permanent, garrison must have bolstered the fledgling-economy of the settlement in the same way that garrison-towns today are dependent on the fortunes of their soldiery.

As military activity in the region wound down, as conquest changed to administrative control, it is likely that the need to store or move large quantities of supplies around also diminished. This might suggest that with the end of active campaigning, Ribchester could have undergone a dramatic change, from distribution-depot to local government administrative centre,[25] resulting in the abandonment of the industrial buildings to the north of the fort.

The fort, rather unusually, appears to have remained occupied until the end of the Roman period. As the defences of the fort were altered through the second and third centuries, so was its interior. Excavation of the *principia*, two granaries, and the western gateway[26] have established a sequence of rebuilds and major reconstructions dated to AD 150–200, and to the early third century, the latter perhaps undertaken by the sixth legion.[27] With the abandonment of the area north of the fort, perhaps never in residential use, the focus of the settlement appears to have shifted eastwards, with the bath-house, broadly dated to the second century,[28] remaining in use during the third. Such a reorientation is not unknown in other Roman extra-mural settlements,[29] and perhaps reflects the changing emphasis of the settlement, away from the fort and soldiery.

Evidence suggests that during the later second, and early to mid-third centuries the settlement enjoyed an enhanced status. Excavations in 1980[30] and 1993[31] discovered a large, defensive rampart and ditch, ostensibly surrounding the northern periphery of the town, which was dated to this period. Although not unknown in England, defences enclosing areas of extra-mural settlement are rare, and though they may have been built for a number of reasons – fear of attack, delimitation, or civic pride – their rarity implies that, whatever the reasons behind their construction, defended 'civil' settlements were of special status.

Epigraphic and literary evidence are, however, our clearest evidence of special status. Two inscriptions are particularly important; the first,[32] on a dedication-slab dated to AD 225–35, implies that the garrison-commander had an unusually broad remit, over a wide area. The second[33] on the shaft of a rectangular pedestal, bearing reliefs of Apollo, and two female figures personifying *Regio Bremetenacenis* and *Britannia Inferior*, testifies to the presence at Ribchester of a *numerous equitatum Sarmatorum*, Sarmatian auxiliaries from Eastern Europe. Marcus Aurelius is thought to have brought a troop of 5,500 Sarmatian cavalry to Britain in AD 175,[34] and it is generally thought that this inscription refers to a veteran settlement for these men and their families. Although non-legionary veteran settlements are rare, the Roman name for Ribchester, *Bremetenacum Veteranorum*, leaves little doubt of its status. Other literary references have come to light recently,[35] but three well known references in the Antonine Itinerary, the *Notitia Dignitatum*, the *Ravenna Cosmography*,[36] must imply that the settlement was both well known and worthy of remark.

Although there is little evidence for activity within the fort during the fourth century, coins and pottery dated around AD 367, must imply that some occupation continued throughout the period. If, indeed, the fort remained in use into the fourth century, as is implied by the construction of a wide, flat bottomed defensive ditch some distance from the rampart at that date, then surely some repair would have proved necessary to buildings a century old.

No discussion of Ribchester is complete without a mention of what is not known about the site. Two possible temples are implied by inscriptions; the first, probably not an official building, was dedicated to Apollo Maponus[37] (the same inscription which mentioned Sarmatian troops); the second was probably dedicated to Jupiter Dolichenos.[38] Both must have been somewhere outside the fort, in the extra-mural settlement. The whereabouts of the cemetery also remains unknown. Law and tradition dictated that it should lie outside the settlement, presumably flanking one of the main arterial roads. Although some tombstones have been found, including one from the river showing an Asturian cavalryman, and cremation-burials are known from the centre of the modern village, the main cemetery has yet to be found.

In addition, although Ribchester's third- and fourth-century history are known from other sources, little physical or material evidence of this date has, as yet, been excavated. Still less is known of its development in the fifth century and later, as the settlement slowly evolved into the Ribchester of today.

Despite such gaps in the record, however, the story of Roman Ribchester is well-known in comparison with other Roman sites in the north-west; but it is worth stressing how many blank pages remain. There are still numerous, widespread and well-preserved

Roman deposits remaining beneath the village and it has been established that even in areas of modern disturbance,[39] significant Roman deposits can survive. Modern techniques, and an integrated approach, using specialists from many different disciplines, can, as recent work[40] has demonstrated, recover considerable information from even small excavations in the village. Without this small scale work, alongside large excavations, the story of Ribchester cannot be fully unfolded, each small site adding its brush-stroke to the ever growing picture of life in *Bremetenacum Veteranorum* and in the province beyond.

Notes

1. Edwards (1981).
2. Buxton and Howard-Davis, forthcoming (a). This is the full report of the excavations of 1980 and 1989–90.
3. A. C. H. Olivier and R. C. Turner, 'Excavations in advance of sheltered housing accommodation, Parsonage Avenue, Ribchester, 1980', in Edwards and Webster (1987), pp. 55–80.
4. Buxton and Howard-Davis, forthcoming.
5. Buxton and Howard-Davis, forthcoming.
6. Buxton and Howard-Davis, forthcoming.
7. S. Stallibrass, 'The Animal-bone', in Buxton and Howard-Davis, forthcoming (a).
8. J. Huntley, 'The Plant-remains', in Buxton and Howard Davis, forthcoming (a).
9. Shotter (1993).
10. Buxton and Howard-Davis, forthcoming (b).
11. Wilson (1980).
12. B. J. N. Edwards, P. V. Webster, G. D. B. Jones and J. P. Wild, 'Excavation on the western defences and in the interior, 1970', in Edwards and Webster (1985), pp. 19–40.
13. Buxton and Howard-Davis, forthcoming (a).
14. B. J. N. Edwards, *et al* (as in footnote 12).
15. B. J. N. Edwards, *et al* (as in footnote 12).
16. *RIB* 583 and 587.
17. Buxton and Howard-Davis, forthcoming (a); B. J. N. Edwards and P. V. Webster, 'Trial Excavations in the Playing-fields car park, 1973', in Edwards and Webster (1987), pp. 81–3; B. J. N. Edwards, G. D. B. Jones and P. V. Webster, 'Trial Excavations in the Playing-Fields, 1968–9', in Edwards and Webster (1987), pp. 13–27; Olivier and Turner (1987), as in footnote 3.
18. Edwards (1981).
19. D. Starley, 'The Industrial residues', in Buxton and Howard-Davis, forthcoming (a).
20. C. L. E. Howard-Davis, 'The Copper-alloy and The Leather', in Buxton and Howard-Davis, forthcoming (a).
21. *RIB* 586.
22. *RIB* 583.

23. Howard-Davis (as in footnote 20).
24. K. M. Buxton and C. L. E. Howard-Davis, 'Ribblesdale Mill, 1990', in Buxton and Howard-Davis, forthcoming (a).
25. Suggested by *RIB* 587.
26. G. Simpson, 'Ribchester Roman Fort: its historical outline supplemented by the decorated samian pottery', in Edwards and Webster (1985), pp. 9–17.
27. *RIB* 591.
28. Smith (1975); Godwin (1978 and 1980).
29. M. J. Jones (1977).
30. Olivier and Turner (as in footnote 3).
31. Time-Team (1994), *On the Northern Frontier* (Channel Four).
32. *RIB* 587.
33. *RIB* 583.
34. Edwards (1981).
35. Bowman (1994).
36. Rivet and Smith (1979).
37. *RIB* 583.
38. *RIB* 587.
39. Buxton and Howard-Davis (as in footnote 24).
40. R. J. Hill and K. M. Buxton, *The White Bull Hotel, Ribchester: Report on the Roof-survey and watching brief* (submitted to clients, 1994); N. R. J. Neil and K. M. Buxton, *Fort Avenue, Ribchester: Archaeological Watching brief* (submitted to client, 1995).

References to Introductory Essays

Birley, R. N., *Vindolanda: A Roman Frontier on Hadrian's Wall* (1977).
Bowman, A. K., *Life and Letters on the Roman Frontier* (1994).
Buxton, K. M., and Howard-Davis, C. L. E., *Ribchester Excavations 1980, 1989–90* (forthcoming).
Edwards, B. J. N., 'Roman Finds from "Contrebis"', *CW²*, LXXI (1971), 17–33.
Edwards, B. J. N., *Ribchester: Lancashire* (Ribchester, 1981).
Edwards, B. J. N. and Webster, P. V., *Ribchester Excavations: Excavations within the Fort* (Cardiff, 1985).
Edwards, B. J. N. and Webster, P. V., *Ribchester Excavations: Excavations in the Civil Settlement* (Cardiff, 1987).
Godwin, E., 'Excavations at the Roman Bath-house, Ribchester', *Lancashire Arch. Bull.*, IV(4) (1978).
Godwin, E., 'Excavations at the Roman Bath-house, Ribchester', *Lancashire Arch. Bull.*, V(6) (1980).
Jones, G. D. B., *Roman Manchester* (Altrincham, 1974).
Jones, G. D. B. and Shotter, D. C. A., *Roman Lancaster* (Manchester, 1988).
Jones, M. J., *Roman Fort Defences to AD 117* (Oxford, 1975), BAR No. 21.
Jones, M. J., 'Archaeological Work at Brough-under-Stainmore, 1971–72, *CW²*, LXXVII (1977), pp. 17–47.
Penney, S. H., *Lancaster: The Evolution of its Townscape to 1800* (Lancaster, 1981).
Richmond, I. A., 'Roman Leaden Sealings from Brough-under-Stainmore, *CW²*, XXXVI (1936), pp. 194–25.
Rivet, A. L. F. and Smith, C., *The Place-Names of Roman Britain* (1979).
Shotter, D. C. A., 'Numeri Barcariorum: A Note on *RIB* 601', *Britannia* IV (1973), pp. 206–9.
Shotter, D. C. A., 'Rome and the Brigantes: Early Hostilities', *CW²*, XCIV (1994), pp. 21–34.
Shotter, D. C. A., and White, A. J., *The Roman Fort and Town of Lancaster* (Lancaster, 1990).
Smith, S., 'Excavation in the Garden of the White Bull, Ribchester, 1975', *Ribble Archaeological Society*, VII (1975).
Watkin, W. T., *Roman Lancashire* (Liverpool, 1883).
Wilson, R. J. A., *Roman Forts* (Aylesbury, 1980).

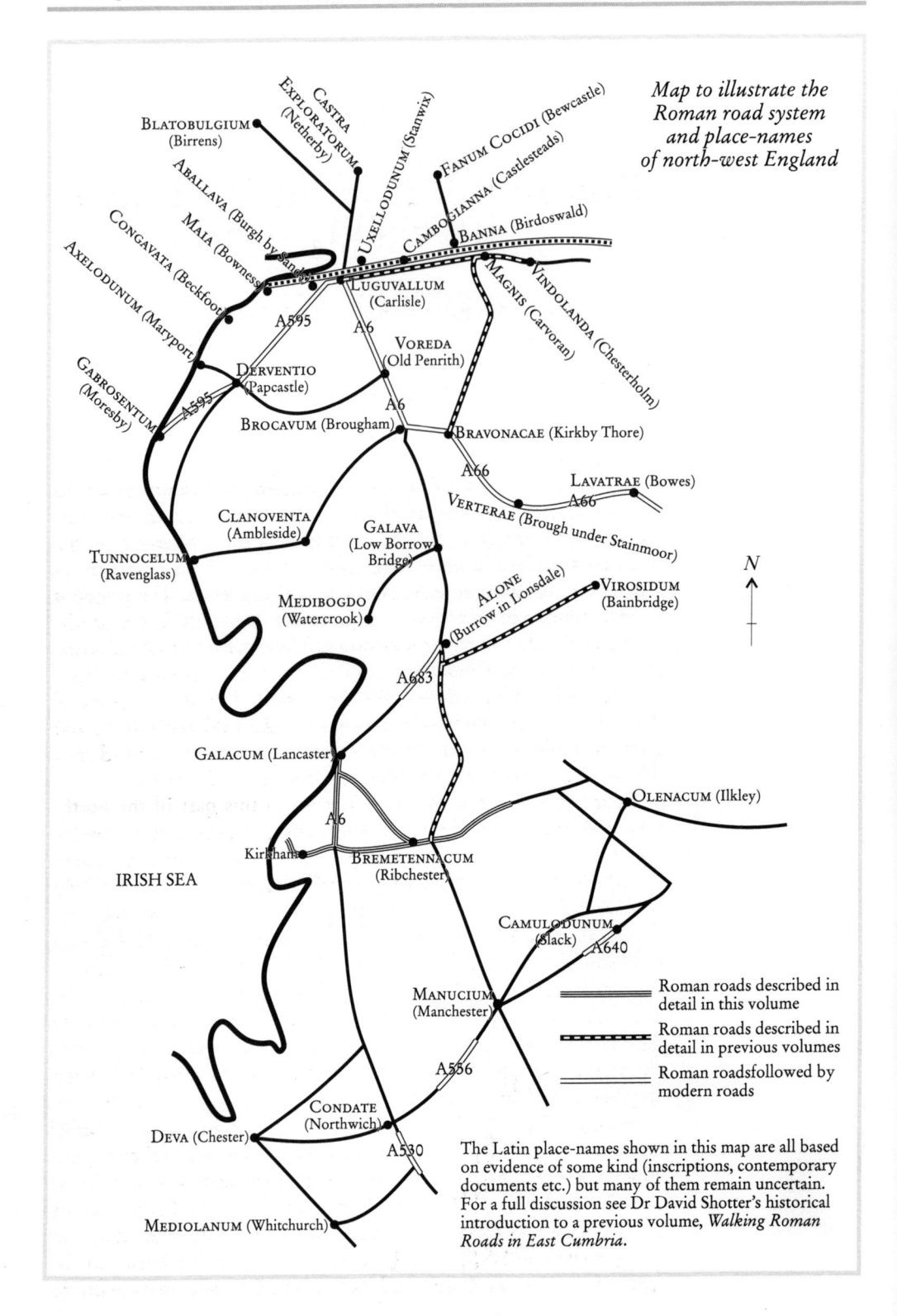

Walking Roman Roads in the Fylde and Ribble Valley

Map to illustrate the Roman road system and place-names of north-west England

The Latin place-names shown in this map are all based on evidence of some kind (inscriptions, contemporary documents etc.) but many of them remain uncertain. For a full discussion see Dr David Shotter's historical introduction to a previous volume, *Walking Roman Roads in East Cumbria*.

Part 1

Roman Roads in the Fylde and in the Ribble Valley: a general survey

Philip Graystone

For the purposes of this book I have taken the Fylde to mean the Lancashire plain bordered by the Ribble on the south, the Lune on the north, the Irish Sea on the west and the mountains on the east. To this I have added the Ribble Valley as far upstream as Downham, some three miles north-east of Clitheroe. The principal Roman centres of this chosen region were Lancaster in the north-west and Ribchester in the south-east. These were two of the many forts whereby the Romans controlled the largely military territory which would later become north-west England. In the hierarchy of Roman strong points they would have ranked relatively high, and they were the hinges of the road system of the area. A third fort, whose role is less well understood, was sited at Kirkham.

Four major Roman roads are known in this part of the north-west; two may be considered as beginning and ending in the region; the two others form part of longer roads starting or terminating elsewhere. The roads belonging entirely to the region are, firstly the road directly connecting Ribchester and Lancaster, secondly the road leading westwards from Ribchester to Kirkham and thence (probably) to Poulton-le-Fylde and to the coast in the Wyre estuary. Of roads in the second category, the first is the northern part of the route from what is now Cheshire and south Lancashire, crossing the Ribble at Preston and continuing north to Lancaster. The second is the western section of the road from Ribchester eastwards through the Aire gap to Ilkley and York.

Both the Fylde and the Ribble valley are largely areas either of urban development or of farmland; there is little of the uncultivated moorland which is such a feature of the Pennine area, Bowland Forest and the Lake District. So the Roman roads of the Fylde and the Ribble valley – though possibly just as numerous as those of other north- western areas – have left fewer visible traces on the ground. Quite often other clues must be sought – references in earlier writings, for example, or place names, whether of villages, farms, or even fields. Tracing Roman roads in this way can be almost as fascinating as following their visible remains on the ground, though not, of course, as rewarding for the outdoor walking enthusiast.

Some place names are obvious pointers to the proximity of a Roman road – the word 'street', for example, whether alone or combined (perhaps in an altered form) with another word e.g. Stratford, Stratton. 'Street' is the modern version of the Old English 'straet' meaning specifically a Roman road; it may well have been picked up by the Anglo-Saxons on the Continent before coming to England. The metalling of the Roman roads was in sharp contrast to the simple tracks of the early settlers, and hence the adjective 'stony' (stony lane etc) is often a pointer to a Roman route. A common word for a road, especially in the north, is 'gate', from Old Norse 'gata', and this, especially when combined with derivatives of 'stone' (e.g. 'stanegate' and the like) is another indication. Other less certain evidence is supplied by names, generally of farms, of the type 'Cold Harbour' or 'Windy Arbour'. These, according to Ekwall (1964), often refer to unheated roadside shelters for travellers, and since most of the through routes in early times were Roman, such shelters would often be found alongside them.

The foreword has already emphasised that the purpose of the rough sketch maps is not to guide the walker but simply to indicate the approximate whereabouts of features mentioned in the text. Here is should be added that very frequently, in the Fylde especially, the exact courses of Roman roads have not been established, so that the routes shown on the sketch maps must be considered as probable only. Attention is generally drawn to this in the accompanying text.

Part 2

The Roman Road from Ribchester to Lancaster

Section One:
Over Longridge Fell

(OS Pathfinder nos. 680, 679: Landranger No. 102)

Though hardly the most interesting – or indeed best authenticated – Roman road in the area, this route is the first to be described since it joins up the two most important centres, Lancaster in the north and Ribchester in the south. David Shotter and Katharine Buxton have given detailed and scholarly accounts of both places in their introductory essays, and nothing needs to be added here.

It nay be appropriate, however, before setting out along this first road, to list some of the things we shall be looking for. In the introduction the importance of place names originating in earlier times has already been noted, and in fact our forefathers have left us other important clues. When the Anglo-Saxons arrived in England, they did not find the Roman roads of much use as long-distance means of communication, since they tended to settle in self-sufficient communities. But with their straight alignments and (at that time) bold profile, the Roman roads formed convenient lines of demarcation. Hence it is still quite common to find them marking the boundaries of parishes and estates (sometimes even counties). Above all it is especially common to find them followed by field boundaries – hedges and walls. Occasionally, of course, they are followed by main roads – though this is not very common in north-west England – and frequently by farm-tracks and footpaths. The Romans normally built their roads on a raised ridge (the Latin word is *agger*, a term often used nowadays in writing about these roads), and traces of this, albeit flattened and damaged, often survive, together with signs of the ditches which usually ran along each side for drainage. Finally, the presence of engineered features, such as terraceways and cuttings, on an ancient road, is often a clue to a Roman origin. All these signs, with others that will be noted from time to time, will be met with in travelling the Fylde roads.

Walking Roman Roads in the Fylde and Ribble Valley

From Ribchester to Back Lane

(Right) Metalling exposed in the south bank of the stream which crosses the Roman line near Gill Bridge.

(Below) Looking north along the ridge, marked by a lighter growth of grass, which runs just west of the B6245 as it leaves Ribchester. The fence on the right marks the modern road.

Part 2

In view of the fact that Ribchester and Lancaster were the two principal Roman military centres in the area, it is surprising that no trace is found, on the 1991 edition of the O.S. map of Roman Britain, of any road directly joining them. This probably reflects doubt about the route rather than about the actual existence of the road, since it would have been remarkable if two such important and neighbouring forts were not so linked. Authors such as Margary (1957) certainly include the road in their survey, though Margary makes the reservation that the exact course is for some distance uncertain.

However the first mile or so, starting from Ribchester, seems to be clearly indicated by the very straight stretch of the Preston road (B 6245) heading north-west from the village; in fact this section is marked 'Roman Road' on earlier editions of the O.S. Landranger map of the area. In the fields on the west side of this road a ridge runs parallel to it, from a point opposite New House onwards to Singleton House, quite clearly marked just inside the hedge, indicating that the modern road is running alongside the Roman line throughout this stretch.

Beyond Higher Alston the road starts to wind somewhat and would appear to mark the line only approximately. Then about 300 yards to the north of Buckley Gate the B 6245 turns sharply south-west (an inn stands on the corner) and a side road leading northwards by Ward Hall continues the line. This section is again by no means straight, but it should be noted that the very steep gradients encountered in crossing Page Brook may well have caused local deviations in the Roman alignment. In fact the road straightens out again before crossing Knowle Green Road (B 6243) and then continues as the approach lane to Written Stone Farm – very straight and occupying a narrow strip in a relatively wide space between the hedges –

Looking south from Written Stone Farm. The road is very straight, with a wide verge, especially on its eastern side.

Written Stone Lane as it nears Green Banks – quite wide, though not raised.

a frequent sign of age in a road. This section certainly shows signs of a Roman origin.

For 300 yards or so beyond the farm Written Stone Lane continues on the same line, now commencing the ascent of Longridge Fell. The hill is steep, though quite often Roman roads are not deterred by even steeper gradients, and in fact a series of field walls continues the straight line on to the summit. However there is no other trace of the road along this line, and Written Stone Lane itself swings to the west and pursues a slanting course up the fell. Margary considers that the lane continues to indicate the probable line of the Roman road – slanting to ease the gradient. If so, it must have changed its character greatly, for it becomes very narrow – only a yard or two between the hedges – and also deeply sunken (and incidentally, very muddy when the weather is at all wet). However, as the lane approaches Green Banks it widens considerably and presents much more the appearance of a road which could have originated in Roman times.

Shortly afterwards the lane reaches a reservoir, which obscures any further trace, on this line at any rate, as the summit of the fell is approached. On the northern slopes of the fell Margary suggests that the line might again have followed a slanting course, coinciding in this instance with the lane that now descends Birks Brow. This however would not fit in well with the subsequent course of the road further down, at least as it was described by earlier writers (e.g. Jackson, 1897, and Codrington, 1918). Their starting point was near the Derby Arms Inn, which still stands on the road running S W to N E on the lower slopes of the fell and marked as Longridge Road on Pathfinder 680. The course of the Roman road could well lie to the west of, and parallel to, the lane which leaves Longridge road in a

The ridge crossing the field north of Withinreap Farm.

Looking east along the hedge which continues the line to the point where the modern road rejoins it at a right-angled bend south of Holwood House. (Taken from this bend.) Longridge Fell in the background.

north-west direction at the point where the Derby Arms stands. Certainly there seem to be signs of a ridge in the little copse in the angle of road and lane, and traces of this also in the field to the north west.

About a quarter of a mile further on, near Priest Hill, the lane swings on to this line, and eventually continues it to near Hill House, following a straight course and (much further on) being marked as Back lane on the Pathfinder map (No. 668). Before this, however, the lane leaves the Roman line just before reaching the river Loud at Gill Bridge and bends sharply to the north, returning to the line beyond Holwood. (This small section, rather inconveniently, is in the corner of Pathfinder Map No. 679). It is an important deviation for our purposes, for in the fields which intervene a ridge can be plainly seen continuing the line. The ridge crosses the field north of Withinreap Farm, and at the western edge arrives at a brook, in the west bank of which road metalling is clearly visible on the same line. On the west side of the stream a hedge then follows the line until the modern lane rejoins it, just to the south of Holwood.

Buckley Gate, on the line of the road about a mile and a half north-west of Ribchester, and Moss Gate, just north-west of the Derby Arms, are place-names which might refer to the road; Written Stone, of course, refers to the prominent inscription at this farm and has nothing to do with the road. It is regrettable that so much of the course across Longridge Fell is uncertain. The route suggested by Margary does seem unnecessarily deviating. Codrington mentions an 'ancient causeway' across the Fell, though he is somewhat vague about details, and there is a direct track via Dilworth Brows and Stone Croft which looks interesting on the map, though less so on the ground. This is certainly an area where future exploration might well prove fruitful.

Note on access. The only parts of this section not followed by (minor) roads are Written Stone Lane, and the stretch from near Gill Bridge to south of Holwood. However footpaths (with right of way) follow the line in both cases, so there is no problem with access. There are, indeed, other interesting tracks in the area of uncertainty on the summit of the fell. For example, a very direct path, with public access, leads from Written Stone Lane across the summit via Dilworth Brows and Stone Croft to Birks Brow. On the northern side other tracks – some with right of way – run in the right direction in the neighbourhood of Little Town and Hill Top. My own investigation of these by-ways has so far been unfruitful, but others may have been, or may prove to be, more successful.

Section Two
From Holwood to Stangyule

(Pathfinder nos. 679, 668: Landranger no. 102)

THE last chapter concluded with the lane rejoining the Roman line just south of Holwood. This lane, which continues the line very directly, is known as 'Back Lane' further along its course (on Pathfinder map No. 668), and it will be convenient to refer to it by this name. After running very straight, with quite wide verges, for almost a mile beyond Weathercock farm, it changes its direction more to the west and winds considerably while keeping to the same general alignment. A glance at the map overleaf will show that the route which, in the author's opinion, was followed by the Roman road for the next few miles will include the straight section of Back Lane already referred to, then the equally straight stretch of Church Lane which runs past Whitechapel, and finally the very direct road which runs almost due north to Middle Lickhurst, all connected by short links not now followed by roads or paths. This route is of course by no means certain, but there is evidence supporting it, which we now proceed to set out.

In the first place Church Lane and the Middle Lickhurst road are considered by such an eminent authority as Margary as likely Roman alignments . The sketch map overleaf (or, better still, Pathfinder No. 668) will show how these stretches skirt the lower slopes of Beacon Fell – a considerable obstacle. The avoidance of difficult territory by a series of straight alignments rather than a curving path is a typical Roman stratagem. Finally there is some evidence for the line across country in the gap between the north-western end of the Back Lane stretch and the south-eastern end of the Church Lane stretch. If we start at the north-western end of this gap, i.e. on Church Lane, at the point where the lane to Fell Side leads off to the north-east, we can distinguish a distinct ridge on the north side of Church Lane just before this turn off. This ridge points south-east past the farm called Ashes towards the western end of Back Lane. It goes first through a small roadside copse and makes a hump in the Fellside path which it then crosses. It ends abruptly at the edge of the next field, as if deliberately levelled, but first crosses a field-side ditch in which boulders appear at the crossing point.

The sketch map on page 30 will perhaps clarify this rather

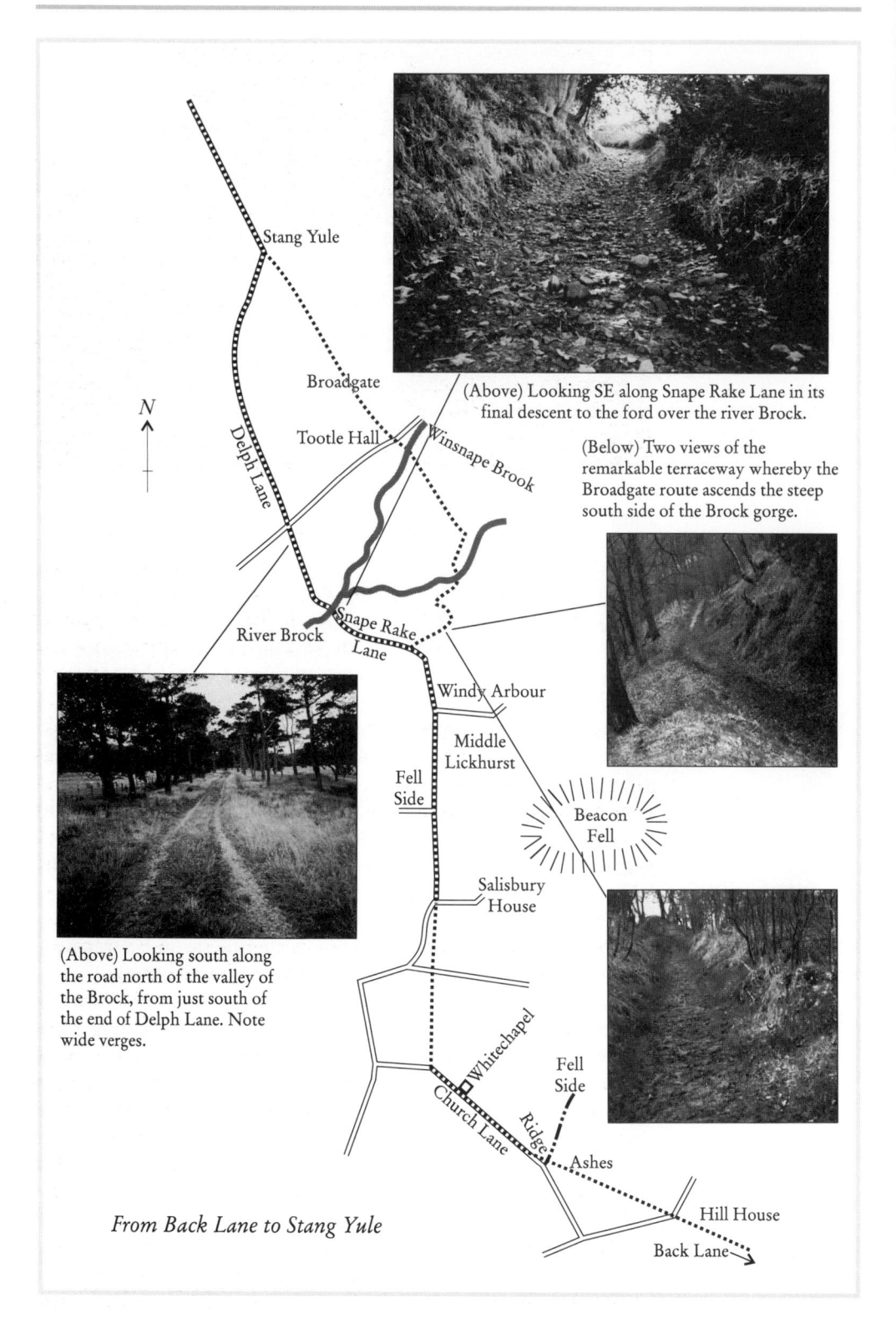

Walking Roman Roads in the Fylde and Ribble Valley

(Above) Looking SE along Snape Rake Lane in its final descent to the ford over the river Brock.

(Below) Two views of the remarkable terraceway whereby the Broadgate route ascends the steep south side of the Brock gorge.

(Above) Looking south along the road north of the valley of the Brock, from just south of the end of Delph Lane. Note wide verges.

From Back Lane to Stang Yule

30

Looking south-east along the ridge described in the text. Church Lane is on the right; the hedge ahead shows where the path to Fell Side crosses.

complex description. It must be emphasised that the Roman origin of this ridge is hypothetical only. Excavation might perhaps settle the problem; meanwhile we have here a feature which adds probability to our suggested route. No similar features are apparent between the northern end of the straight section of Church Lane and the southern end of the straight section of the Middle Lickhurst road.

The next interesting section commences north of Middle Lickhurst, where the present road makes a right angled turn and heads off east towards Higher Lickhurst and beyond. The Roman line, continuing straight on, is now approaching the deep gorge of the river Brock, where a diversion to a suitable crossing point might be expected. Different routes have been suggested to the river and beyond. The one first described here follows the minor road shown on Pathfinder No. 668 as Snape Rake Lane, which curves to the west to cross the river just downstream of its confluence with a tributary, Winsnape Brook, thus ensuring one crossing instead of two.

Snape Rake Lane, on its approach to the Brock, passes close to a site shown on older maps as Windy Arbour, an interesting name discussed earlier, in the introduction. It descends the steep valley through deep cuttings as a narrow, heavily metalled lane, winding to ease the gradient and ending at what was once evidently an old ford across the river, replaced now by a footbridge. The ascent of the north bank follows a similar pattern, and on reaching higher ground the road appears as straight narrow track in a broad green strip between ditches some fifteen yards apart.

Delph Lane now comes on to the line with a sharp bend to the north west and follows an almost straight course for about a mile before swinging to just east of north. In nearly half a mile the farm

Snape Rake Lane commencing its ascent of the north bank immediately after leaving the ford over the river Brock.

called Stang Yule is reached. Formerly it had the very significant name of Stangate or Stanygate, and there is general agreement that it stands on the Roman line (Codrington, 1918; Jackson, 1897; Leather, 1972), which now turns north west and is followed by the present road.

As indicated earlier, another suggestion has been made for the part of the route described above. It will be convenient to investigate this by going southwards from Stang Yule to the River Brock and beyond to Snape Rake lane. This alternative route is favoured by Jackson, Margary, seemingly, and Leather, though Leather does not discount the route we have followed earlier. It is also favoured by Gordon Heald, who has made a thorough investigation of the area and has kindly sent me the results.

This second route would lead south-eastwards from Stang Yule, continuing more closely the alignment followed to the north of the farm. At first sight the very striking continuous line of field walls from Stang Yule to Broadgate, showing up so conspicuously on Pathfinder No. 668, looks attractive, but closer inspection shows that this line follows the bottom of a quite steep-sided little valley; not a typical route for a Roman road. The route would probably lie further to the east, possibly represented by the track shown on the O.S. one-inch Landranger map (though not on the Pathfinder), and following higher ground on a parallel course. The route must have passed close by Broadgate Farm, a name frequently associated with Roman roads, and thereafter probably swerved west to coincide with the track from Broadgate Farm to the minor road at Tootle Hall. South of Tootle Hall the signs become more evident; a prominent ridge with side ditches appears on the line in the first field. Still more impressive are the cuttings which ease the gradient north and south

Looking north along the ridge in the field south-east of Tootle Hall; note the distinct signs of a ditch on its left (west) side.

Looking south along the cutting approaching Winsnape Brook from the south.

of Winsnape Brook. These now lead to an old disused bridge, which may well have replaced an older ford, though there are no very obvious signs of this.

South of the brook the road is still used as a farm track and follows a very direct route to the river Brock, accompanied throughout by field walls with signs of the ridge and occasionally of the metalling. For a short distance is joined by the path connecting Brock Close and Moss Side farms – an interesting example of the way in which a Roman road (if indeed this one is Roman) tends to 'capture' other roads which happen to cross it. It descends the north bank of the very deep and steep gorge of the Brock by long, straight, evenly graded terraceways which show skilful engineering, and ascends the south bank by a well contrived zig-zag. The track then

Part of the impressive terraceway on the northern side of the Brock valley.

The hairpin bend in the terrace on the south side of the Brock valley.

climbs up to meet the route previously described near Windy Arbour in Snape Rake Lane.

This second route shows expert engineering, but involves two stream crossings, whereas the Delph Lane road manages with one. A complication is that parish boundaries – those frequent indications of Roman lines – follow parts of both routes – in the one case, the northern part of Delph Lane, and in the other, close to the line both north and south of Broadgate. However, it could be that we have here two authentic alternative Roman routes, one possibly succeeding the other. It cannot be too strongly emphasised that the Romans, uninhibited by property rights, had absolute freedom in planning their roads, and no doubt frequently used this to improve parts of their system of communication. In this case the suggestion has been put forward by Gordon Heald – in a private communication to the author – that the route via Tootle Hall might be a later variant for commercial traffic – crossing the formidable valley of the Brock by evenly graded terraceways instead of the very steep descent and ascent of the Snape Rake Lane route.

Note on access. The only parts of this section (including both alternative routes) which cannot be either walked or driven are the linking stretches between Back Lane and Church lane and between Church Lane and the lane to Middle Lickhurst, also the track from Stang Yule to Broadgate. All the rest is covered by minor (mostly very minor) roads or by footpaths with right of way.

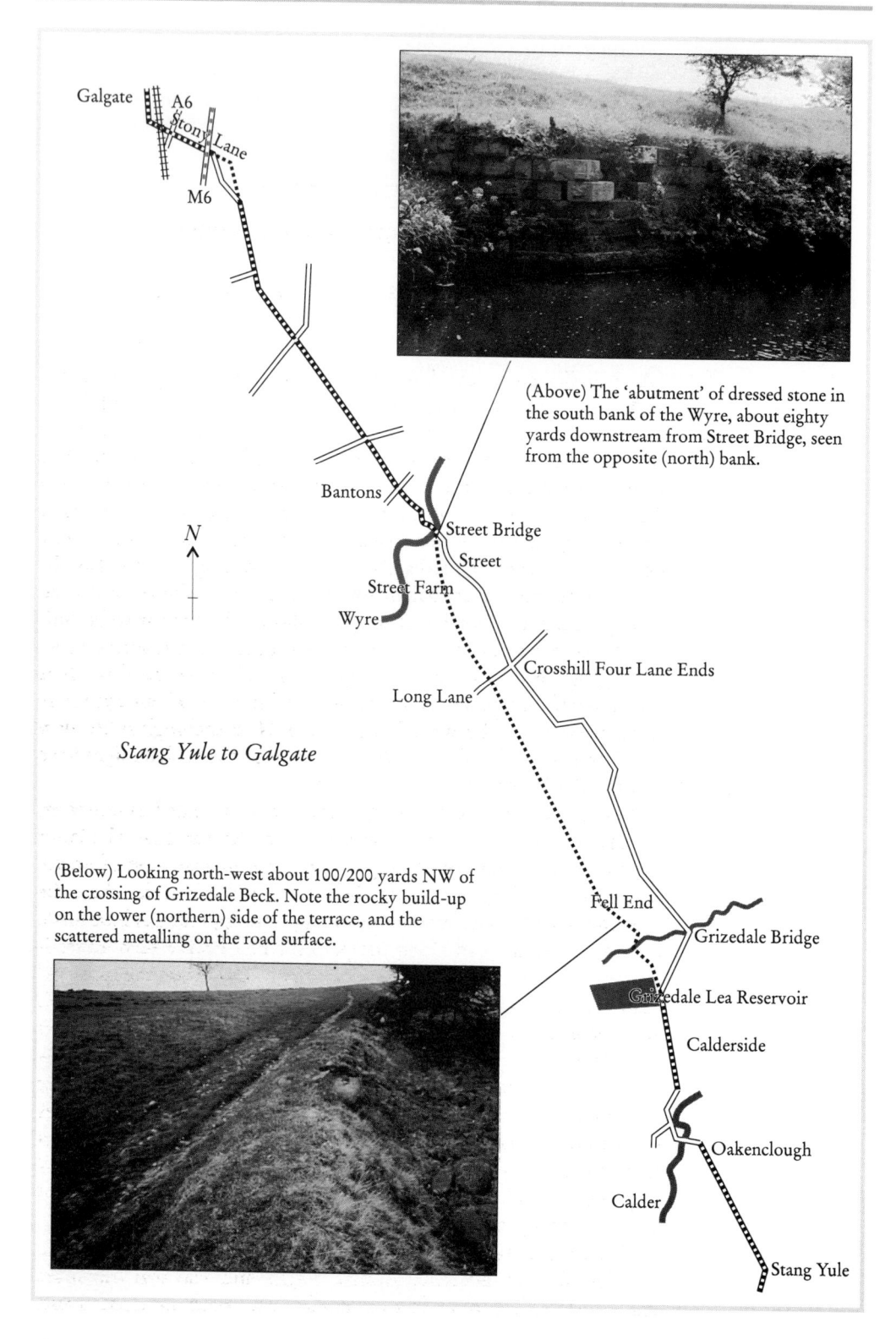

Walking Roman Roads in the Fylde and Ribble Valley

(Above) The 'abutment' of dressed stone in the south bank of the Wyre, about eighty yards downstream from Street Bridge, seen from the opposite (north) bank.

Stang Yule to Galgate

(Below) Looking north-west about 100/200 yards NW of the crossing of Grizedale Beck. Note the rocky build-up on the lower (northern) side of the terrace, and the scattered metalling on the road surface.

Section Three
From Stangyule to Galgate

(Pathfinders Nos. 668, 659: Landranger No. 102)

As indicated in the last chapter, there are strong reasons for supposing that Stang Yule, at the northern end of Delph Lane, lay on or near the Roman line. An additional reason is provided by the commencement here of another parish boundary, which then runs on or close to the present road north-westward to the river Calder, a mile further on. Both Jackson and Leather report signs of the Roman road along this stretch, though I must confess that they do not now seem immediately obvious. Both agree also that the Calder was crossed at Oakenclough, after which the present road swings almost due north and is again followed by the parish boundary. Jackson quotes the then tenant of Calderside, a roadside farm, as digging up a 'good paved road' in an adjoining meadow. It is rather significant, indeed, that Jackson, writing in 1897, always refers to the present road between Stang Yule and Oakenclough as 'the new road', thus implying the existence of an older one which might have marked the Roman line more closely.

In any event the present road, as it passes Grizedale Lea reservoir, swings definitely to the east, away from the Roman line. The latter apparently continues on its alignment, pointing just west of north. It is next met with, on the same line, at Grizedale Brook, where the crossing is visible and worth examining. The approach is best made from the present road along the path (to Fell End) which leaves it westwards at Grizedale Bridge. About 300 yards from the (present) road the track swings north-west (to follow, in fact, the Roman line), and becomes an impressive terrace as it climbs to the north-west away from the stream. Its northern or lower side is built up of stones until the track reaches higher ground in the next field, after which it follows a direct route to Fell End Farm. Retracing one's steps southwards to the actual approach to Grizedale Brook, a final short terraceway is very clear on a different alignment (north-east/south-west), ending on the bank of the stream opposite what could well be a bridge abutment on the south side.

There is general agreement amongst investigators that the section just described is indeed of Roman origin, and also that traces are again met with a mile further north, just south of Long Lane.

(Margary, 1957; Jackson, 1897; Leather, 1972). My own notes indicate a green hollow way, south of Long Lane, and about 150 yards west of the crossroads marked as Crosshill Four Lane Ends on Pathfinder No. 659. This hollow way leads off in the direction of Fell End.

About two thirds of a mile further north the river Wyre is reached, and here a cluster of 'Street' names is encountered; Street Farm, Street Bridge, and the hamlet of Street itself (which may of course have given its name to farm and bridge, but still is in itself significant). All of these lie on or near the (modern) road to Galgate, which crosses the Wyre at Street Bridge.

However there are indications that the Roman road itself may have crossed the river at another nearby point. About eighty yards downstream from Street Bridge an abutment of dressed stone appears in the south bank of the river, noted and commented on by all the observers we have quoted – indeed it is too carefully constructed and well preserved to be overlooked. It looks like a bridge abutment, but opinions differ as to its date. Margary regards it as probably a recent construction – though earlier than the present Street Bridge; Leather refers to Professor Droop who regarded the masonry as Roman, Jackson and Codrington are wisely undecided. But all except Margary regard this feature – ancient or not – as a probable indication of the Roman crossing point. In support of this Jackson describes visible remains of the Roman road leading up to the abutment from the south, and Leather confirms this, speaking of a cobbled surface about twelve feet wide.

My own recent observations indicate that the abutment – if that is what it is – extends along the river bank for some twenty yards, rather more, one would think, than would be needed for a Roman bridge in this location. However I also came upon a hollow way, with metalling, climbing up southwards from the flood plain of the Wyre west of Street farm, which would certainly fit in with a crossing at the point where the supposed abutment is found. Moreover, a straight line from the point where traces were seen south-west of Crosshill Four Lane Ends, passing through the 'abutment' and continued north-westwards, would join the (modern) road to Galgate at Bantons Farm i.e. at the point where it straightens out on an alignment which is continued for 3½ miles.[1]

This alignment commences a section, extending to within half a mile of Galgate, which runs in straight lengths and is generally

---

[1] It was, unfortunately, only after completing this study that I read the valuable article by B. J. N. Edwards in *Contrebis*, 2,2 (1974) p. 24. This certainly gives convincing support to Margary's opinion that the abutment is of recent origin, though it would appear to leave open the possibility that it marks the crossing point of the Roman road.

The road between Street and Galgate, taken north of Bantons; wide, straight and well raised.

raised, characteristics which Margary regards as definitely Roman. After the first three and a half mile stretch, it swings a little towards the north for about half a mile, again keeping very straight, and finally bends somewhat (perhaps leaving the Roman line for a short distance) before turning west to Galgate, again becoming quite direct.

As this last portion enters Galgate it is signed, significantly, 'Stony Lane'. It then turns almost due north along Highland Brow, no doubt indicating that hereabouts it joined up with the north/south Roman road coming up from the Ribble at Preston and continued with it northwards to Lancaster.

Note on access. From Stang Yule north to Oakenclough and beyond the line is followed, at least approximately, by the present road. The crossing of Grizedale Beck and the line onwards to Fell End Farm can be reached by the footpath (with right of way) from Grizedale Bridge to Fell End. From Fell End north to Long Lane there is no public access. However the 'abutment' west of Street Bridge can be reached by the footpath along the north bank of the Wyre, and the section south of this – around Street Farm – is crossed by two paths. North of Street Bridge the probable Roman line is closely followed by modern roads.

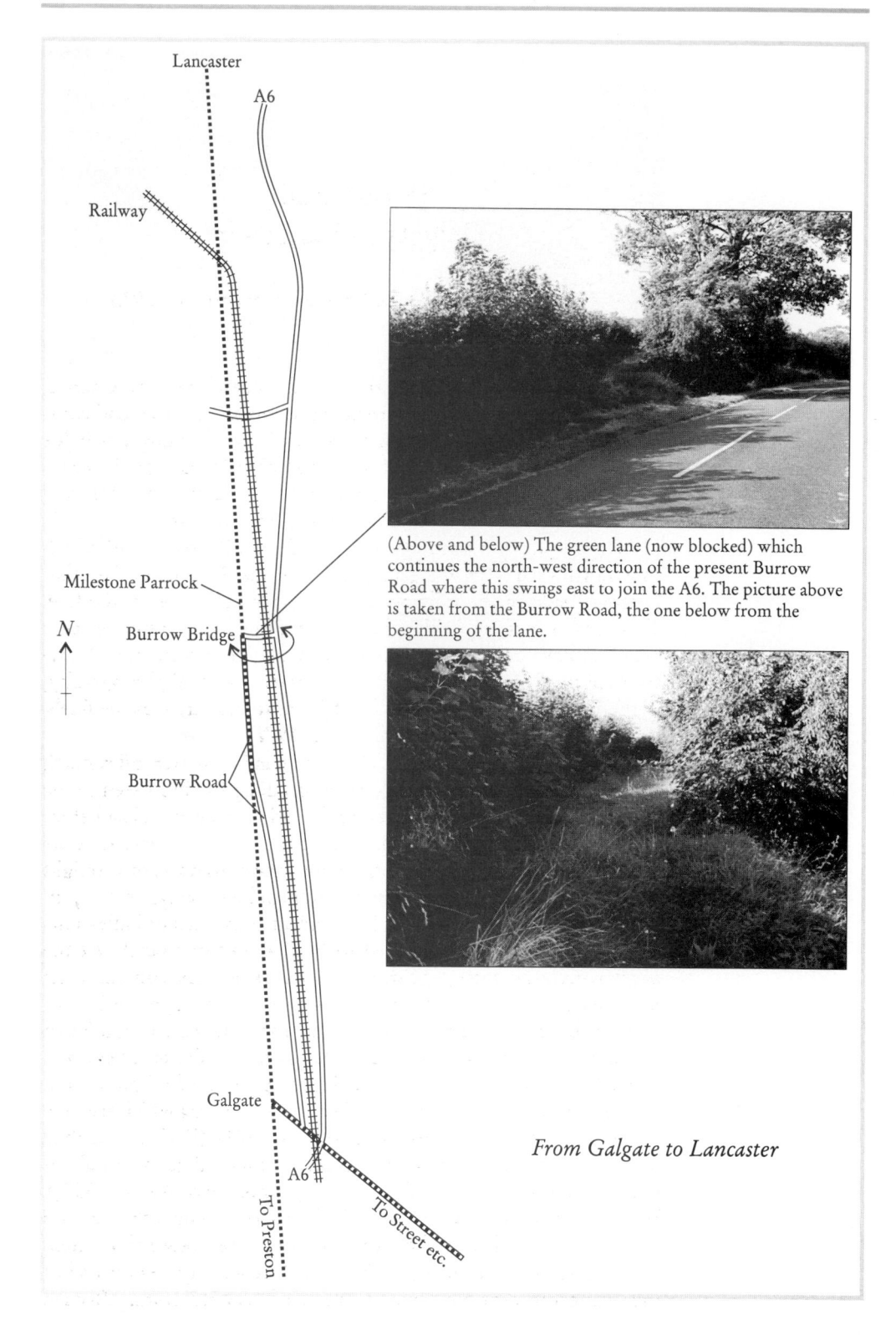

Walking Roman Roads in the Fylde and Ribble Valley

(Above and below) The green lane (now blocked) which continues the north-west direction of the present Burrow Road where this swings east to join the A6. The picture above is taken from the Burrow Road, the one below from the beginning of the lane.

From Galgate to Lancaster

Section Four
Galgate to Lancaster

(Pathfinder nos. 659, 648: Landrangers nos. 102, 97.)

THE last section ended at the point, somewhere near Galgate, where the Ribchester/Lancaster road joined with the road coming up from Preston, the combined road then heading north for Lancaster. Strictly speaking, this last stretch belongs more logically to the Preston/Lancaster road, but we treat of it here to avoid leaving the Ribchester/Lancaster road in mid-course, so to speak.

Margary points to the minor road (the old Burrow road) which runs northward from Galgate, parallel to the A6 but on the other (western) side of the railway, as a probable indication of the line. This road is certainly older than the A6, but in its present state it seems to have originated as an earlier turnpike construction. Some traces of the Roman line have been observed, by aerial photography, slightly to the west of this road, sufficient to indicate it as the likely successor of the Roman road (Leather, 1972).

North of Five Ashes Farm, about one and a quarter miles north of Galgate, a scatter of possible road metalling has been seen in the field – when under plough – west of the old Burrow road, just before this road straightens out on its northerly course, in contrast to its rather curving path further south. After a short distance, this straight section, which seems on or near the Roman line, swings east to join the A6 at Burrow Bridge, but it is evident from further indications that the Roman road continued to head almost due north. At the point where the change of direction occurs, a track continues the previous northerly line of the Burrow road, and though this is now blocked by a hedge after a few yards, the same line is continued intermittently by field boundaries. It passes the site of a field formerly known as 'Milestone Parrock', the probable find point of at least one of the two Roman milestones from this area which are now in the Lancaster City Museum (Edwards, 1971). (Each is inscribed with the name of the reigning emperor, which dates them about midway through the third century. [Shotter and White, 1990]). Because of their size and weight, the find spot in which these stones were redeposited is not likely to be far from their original position.

Another discovery made in the immediate vicinity – at the end of the eighteenth century – was a group of very interesting Roman

The group of statuary from Burrow Heights. (Photograph Geoffrey Harris.)

stone figures. Various explanations have been offered for these; one opinion would regard them as statues from a mausoleum or family tomb; alternatively, perhaps because of their headgear, they have been considered to be figures from a temple of Mithras (Leather, 1972). Like the milestones they can be studied in the Lancaster Museum, which the enthusiast should certainly visit. As far as the road itself is concerned, definite traces have been observed further along the line we have been following, though they are not now to be seen. Kerbstones have been found on the north side of Burrow Beck; further north on Ripley Heights road metalling has been dug up (Leather 1972). In Lancaster itself it has been suggested that the straight line of Penny Street and Cheapside continues the Roman line (Shotter and White,1990); if this is so there must have been a branch road to the fort on Castle Hill. After passing the fort the road is thought to have crossed the Lune and continued on its northern course, quite likely to link up with Watercrook and the forts of the southern Lake District.

Below are given the inscriptions on the two milestones found near the road south of Lancaster and referred to in the text above:

1. 'IMP(eratori) C(aesari) M(arco) IULIO PHILIPPO PIO FEL(ici) AUG(usto) N(ostro)'.
   Translation – For the Emperor Caesar Marcus Julius Philippus Pius Felix, our Augustus. (He reigned AD 244 to 249).

2. 'IMP(eratori) C(aesari) D(omino) N(ostro) GAIO

MESS(io) QUINTO DECIO TRAIANO PIO FELICI INVICTO AUG(usto)'.
Translation – For the Emperor Caesar, Our Lord, Gains Messius Quintus Decius Trajanus Pius Felix Unconquered Augustus (He reigned AD 249 to 251). (Shotter and White, 1990).

(Roman milestones occasionally mention places and distances, but are usually more concerned with displaying the titles of the reigning emperor, as in this instance).

Note on access. In this final approach to Lancaster of the combined roads, from the Ribble at Preston and from Ribchester, there is so little to see in the field that the question of access hardly seems worth pursuing. The reader's best plan would probably be to visit the Lancaster City Museum and inspect the highly interesting milestones and statuary, illustrated above, which have been discovered along or not far from this stretch, as also the various exhibits from Lancaster itself.

Unlike Ribchester, which can boast remains of granaries, baths and ditches, the town itself has virtually nothing to show nowadays of its Roman past; the only trace above ground is the 'Wery Wall', a fragment of masonry in the northern Vicarage Field. Dr Shotter explains in his historical introduction where this fits into Lancaster's Roman history.

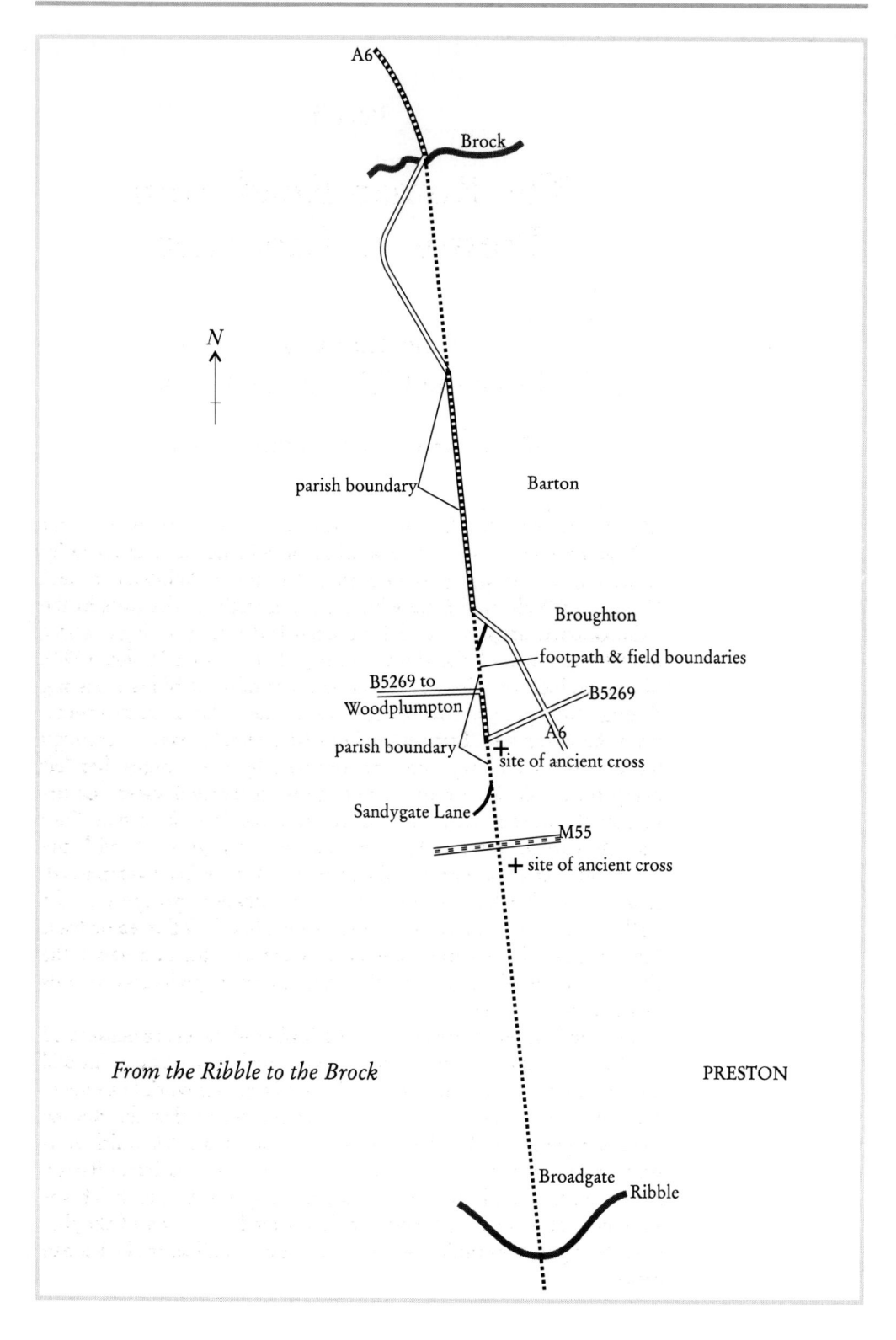

Walking Roman Roads in the Fylde and Ribble Valley

A6

Brock

N

parish boundary

Barton

Broughton

footpath & field boundaries

B5269 to Woodplumpton

B5269

parish boundary

A6

site of ancient cross

Sandygate Lane

M55

site of ancient cross

From the Ribble to the Brock

PRESTON

Broadgate

Ribble

44

Part 3

The Roman Road from Preston to Lancaster

Section One
From the Ribble to the Brock

(Pathfinder no. 679: Landranger no. 102)

A Roman road heading northwards through Preston to Lancaster is marked on the O.S. map of Roman Britain and accepted by all authorities. It was part of a coastal route via Wilderspool and Wigan and Walton-le-Dale which led ultimately to the forts in the Lake district, and may well have been laid out as a single whole towards the end of the third century. (Shotter and White, 1990). However, little remains of the section north of the Ribble i.e. passing through the Fylde, in marked contrast to the earlier northern route, via Ribchester and Burrow-in-Lonsdale, which, passing through more difficult country and not followed by later routes, has left many traces. G. M. Leather gives the most detailed survey of the Preston/Lancaster road, but Codrington dismisses it in nine lines and Margary devotes little more than half a page to it, with the comment that a good part of the route has not yet been ascertained. It is a road that hardly presents a very attractive prospect to the walker: indeed not many sections can be profitably followed on foot. Nevertheless the general comments in the introduction about the Fylde roads hold good here also; and closer acquaintance reveals many points of interest.

For the first few miles north of the Ribble all traces are obliterated by Preston and its suburbs, and perhaps our best starting point will be to study the first certain stretch beyond this and work both north and south from there. There is general agreement that the Roman road is represented by the two-mile section of the A6 which runs past Barton on its west side, from just beyond the crossing of Barton Brook on the south, to Myerscough Cottage on the north. This is an almost straight length and is accompanied for much of the distance by a parish boundary – that very frequent indicator of a Roman route.

If we now continue the Barton alignment southwards from its southern end (see sketch map on page 44) we note that the east-west road to Woodplumpton (B 5269) makes a very abrupt change of direction when it reaches our line from the west and indeed follows it almost due south for a short distance through Broughton, before resuming, equally abruptly, its easterly course. This could well be an example of a phenomenon familiar to students of Roman roads – a more recent road being 'captured' for a short distance by a Roman alignment, with sharp angles where it enters and leaves the alignment. It is a surprisingly common occurrence, certainly common enough to serve as a clue that we are still on the Roman line at this point; a clue reinforced by the fact that on older maps a parish boundary is shown following this diversion and remaining on the same line a short distance northwards to Pope's Farm.

Furthermore, the lane which continues southwards at the southern end of this diversion – following for a short distance approximately the same line until it swings away to the west – is called Sandygate Lane; for the significance of this the reader is referred to the introduction. It is certainly indicative of an old road – not of course, necessarily, of a Roman route, and in any event the lane itself fairly soon bends away from the alignment we have been following. But east of this lane G. M. Leather has observed a mound in the adjacent gardens on the same alignment, and my own notes speak of a low ridge, 1–2ft high but quite broad, running north/south inside the hedge of a field which borders the lane on its eastern side a little further south.

Continuing the Barton line still further southwards – through Preston in fact to the Ribble crossing – brings us to the river in a district called Broadgate, another significant name. On the way the route passes close by the sites of two ancient crosses; one at the northern end of Sandygate lane just referred to, and the other just about four-fifths of a mile further south, not far beyond the M 55, near Lightfoot Lane. The occurrence of such crosses – whether as boundary markers or simply as wayside crosses, is an obvious indicator of antiquity in roads with which they are associated (Taylor, 1902).

In the light of all this we naturally look with interest at the half-mile gap between the northern end of the Broughton diversion and the Barton straight stretch and we note that a footpath links the two and for much of its length follows approximately the same alignment, with field boundaries alongside it, or did until recently. It now appears to have been diverted westwards to follow the stream, though the old stiles were still in place on the author's last visit. The boundaries of two fields still follow the Barton alignment very closely.

The long straight stretch of the A6, beginning just north of Barton Brook and passing northwards through Barton is, as already indicated, generally accepted as on the Roman line. However, just south of Myerscough Cottage, the A6 starts to slant to the west, away from this alignment. The parish boundary continues to follow the A6 on its new line, but the coincidence between road and boundary becomes more approximate; the Pathfinder map no. 679 shows the boundary swinging to the east of the road in places. It is suggested that, where the modern A6 starts to slant westwards, the Roman line continued straight ahead – slightly west of north. The principal reason for this assertion is that, if the previous alignment is continued northwards it will bring us, in about one and a half miles, close to the start of our next suggested Roman alignment, north of the river Brock, and there seems no reason, in the intervening landscape, for the Romans to make any diversion. This is, of course, rather negative; indeed it is at about this point that alternative routes for this road start being proposed, as will be seen in the next chapter.

Note on access. South of Broughton, Sandygate Lane is a track with right of way. North of Broughton to the south end of the 'Barton Straight' public footpaths, again with right of way, follow the line approximately, though with the apparent recent diversion noted in the text above. The remainder of this section is either urban or followed by modern roads, apart from the gap between Myerscough Cottage and the River Brock. Footpaths cross this area near Duncombe, but the earnest seeker should remember that the course of the Roman road hereabouts is by no means certain, and that the construction of the nearby railway might well have obliterated traces.

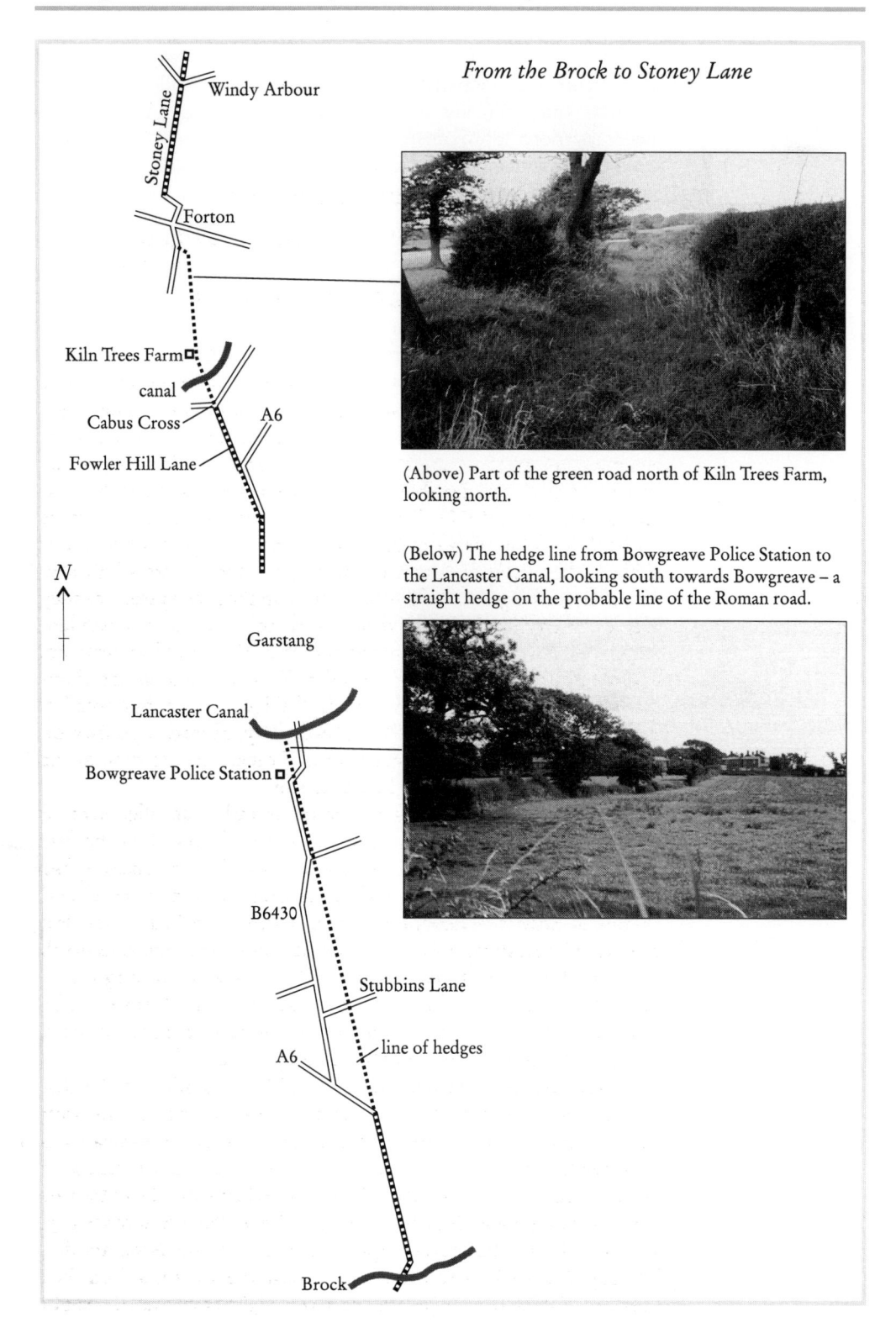

Walking Roman Roads in the Fylde and Ribble Valley

From the Brock to Stoney Lane

(Above) Part of the green road north of Kiln Trees Farm, looking north.

(Below) The hedge line from Bowgreave Police Station to the Lancaster Canal, looking south towards Bowgreave – a straight hedge on the probable line of the Roman road.

Section Two
From the River Brock to Galgate

(Pathfinder 668 & 659: Landranger 102)

In the last chapter the Roman road northwards – or more correctly the approximate line of this road – was followed to a point near Myerscough Cottage on the A6. After a gap in which traces are lacking, exploration again becomes possible, but with the proviso that more than one feasible route has been suggested for the next section (Leather, 1972). To opt for the one which seems more probable is by no means to discount others. To repeat observations made earlier, it is evident that during the long years of Roman occupation changes must have been made in the road system (as they are in our day); rather than repair worn-out stretches the Romans might well have chosen alternative routes, as they could so easily do, having no property rights to consider. This would leave the abandoned sections derelict or in use only by local traffic, but possibly still with traces surviving to the present day. Hence, especially on busy routes, neighbouring stretches of Roman road leading to the same destination should not be unexpected.

The route favoured in this account is rather an alignment of features than of physical remains, and is best followed, in the first instance, on the Pathfinder O.S. map, no. 668. It commences on the A6 just north of the crossing of the river Brock, a point in quite good alignment with the direction further south described in the last chapter. Here a straight stretch of the A6 commences and runs north west for about two thirds of a mile. That this is not of very recent origin (as is the Catterall/Garstang by-pass just ahead) is shown by its appearance on the first edition of the one-inch OS map, for which the survey was made in the 1840s (Harley, 1970).

It has been pointed out (Margary, 1957 & Leather, 1972) that where this straight stretch ends and the A6 swerves to the west (south west of the big bend in the canal) its line northwards is continued, after a short gap, by a series of field boundaries, six or seven in all. These are particularly evident when viewed southwards from Stubbins Lane. North of Stubbins Lane, there is another gap, after which field boundaries again run near the line. After another interruption the B 6430 comes on or near the same line from just north of Calder Bridge (where the river might have caused a slight deviation in the Roman line – if indeed this is the Roman line) to Bowgreave police station. From the police station a hedge continues the line northwards to the Lancaster canal.

This gives a total alignment of just over two and a half miles – significant in view of the fact that both the location and direction fit the road we are studying. The built-up area of Garstang now intervenes, but just north of the town there is a very straight section of the A6 going almost due north for about one third of a mile. It then swings towards the west for a short distance on a line which is taken up, when the A6 bends east again, first by a bridleway and then by the straight line of Fowler Hill Lane. In following this alignment we are on firmer ground; there are definite signs along the way that it is indeed of Roman origin. It should be noted that a large new lay-by now rather obscures the turn-off point of Fowler Hill Lane and may have also obliterated some of the signs of a ridge which were formerly seen hereabouts on the western side of the A6.

Fowler Hill Lane, though quite straight on the map, seems to twist somewhat on the ground; this is quite normal for a Roman route now followed by a minor road; local slight variations of direction occur with continued use and are known as warping. That this is an old road is shown by the ancient wayside cross which stands within the field on its eastern side just before Cabus Cross Roads is reached. Moreover the line is continued straight ahead beyond the crossroads by the lane leading to Kiln Trees Farm, a lane which begins one of the few stretches of this route belonging solely to the walker. On the western side of this lane, a short distance away and parallel to it, a ridge appears which becomes very pronounced as the farm is approached. (Margary calls this a strip – I would say a quite definite ridge).

Before reaching the farm the Lancaster Canal again intervenes, and

Cabus Cross, taken from within the hedge, beyond which is the crossroads.

is crossed by a footbridge, but north of the canal the line is continued by a field boundary, joined quite soon by a footpath with right of way. In the third field north of Kiln Trees Farm an old overgrown road appears on the line of the path for about 200 yards – it is completely derelict and runs between old-looking hedges. It continues almost to the verge of Blackpool stream which the path crosses by a bridge with a stony ford alongside, evidently the crossing of the old road. The footpath, with right of way, continues beyond the stream, heading just west of north. Its general line continues that of Fowler Hill Lane, though it is not entirely straight. Frequently, though not always, it is accompanied by field boundaries. Since there are distinct signs of Roman origin at both ends of this path, some of which we have noted on the way and others which will shortly appear, it seems that it should be considered the general direction, if not the exact course, of the Roman road we are exploring.

The footpath finally emerges on to Park Lane, just south of its junction with the Cockerham/Garstang road. A short distance west of this junction, alongside a gateway opposite Forton Hall Farm, stands a stone which is thought by some investigators to be a Roman milestone. It is uninscribed, but its size and shape would be consistent with a Roman origin and its position near the putative course of a Roman road render this interpretation probable (Edwards, 1969).

Nearby a road heads north with the very significant name of Stoney Lane. After a few yards this swings west and then settles on a straight course, just east of north, which is continued southwards at the bend by a field boundary. To the north the straight stretch of Stoney Lane continues to the canal, and points directly to a farm which, according to the first edition of the one-inch O.S. map, used to be situated just over half a mile ahead and was called Windy Arbour, a name discussed in the introduction. (Harley, 1970). At this point we again lose touch with our route for more than two miles. The Lancaster Canal, which has never been far away, continues to cross and recross the probable line and no doubt is responsible for the loss of many traces. The next probable signs are encountered west of

The stone at Forton, thought to be a Roman milestone.

The derelict road north of Kiln Trees farm.

Galgate, where Margary points to the minor road (the old Burrow road) which runs northward from Galgate, parallel to the A6 but on the other (western) side of the railway, as a probable indication of the line. Hereabouts the Roman road from Ribchester to Lancaster joined the line, and the continuation of the combined roads north to Lancaster has already been covered in an earlier section.

Lack of visible and accessible remains along most of the route from Preston to Lancaster will no doubt disappoint the present-day explorer, especially the walker. The probable reason for this is the use of the Roman route as a north/south thoroughfare throughout the Middle Ages. In the words of one Lancashire historian, for centuries it formed the only communication between the south of the county and Lancaster and Carlisle. (Watkin, 1883). So it is not unexpected to find much of it incorporated into the modern road system, either in the shape of roads actually following its line, like the main road through Barton, or others running in the same direction close alongside, like the old Burrow road. Add to this the excavation involved in constructing the Lancaster Canal, which lies near or across the line from north of Barton onwards, and it is not surprising that so very little survives unscathed.

Much of the interest in tracing a road like this (though again, of little moment to the walker) is the use made of place names along the route. In this case we have come across Broadgate, Sandygate, Stoney Lane, Windy Arbour and (in the section north of Galgate) Milestone Parrock; each of them on its own would be of small moment, but occurring on the same line (or series of alignments) they assume a real significance. This is emphasised by the location of the stone at Forton, certainly resembling a Roman milestone in its size and shape, and situated on the same general line; also by the occurrence of the sites of the two wayside crosses shown on the sketch map for section one, and of Cabus cross in section two.

Note on access. The section followed in this chapter commences on the A6 just north of the Brock, but this road is far too busy for the walker to follow – or for the motorist to pause and survey. Hence when the A6 swerves to the west after about 1200 yards, the line of hedges which is thought to continue the alignment is best surveyed from a quieter vantage point; this can be found by continuing along the A6 and then turning right along Stubbins Lane. Further north, beyond Bowgreave Police Station, the hedge line can be seen from the south bank of the canal. As noted above, access to Fowler Hill Lane is gained from a large new lay-by on the A6; it is a quiet road and at its northern end the old cross at Cabus cross roads is seen across the hedge. Tracks with right of way continue the line beyond Kiln Trees farm all the way to Forton, where the stone, thought to be a Roman milestone, can be seen by the gateway opposite Forton Hall Farm. Stoney lane, which continues the line north after a short break, is a quiet by-road; the gap which follows northwards to Galgate is crossed by tracks along which the enthusiastic explorer might venture in search of clues.

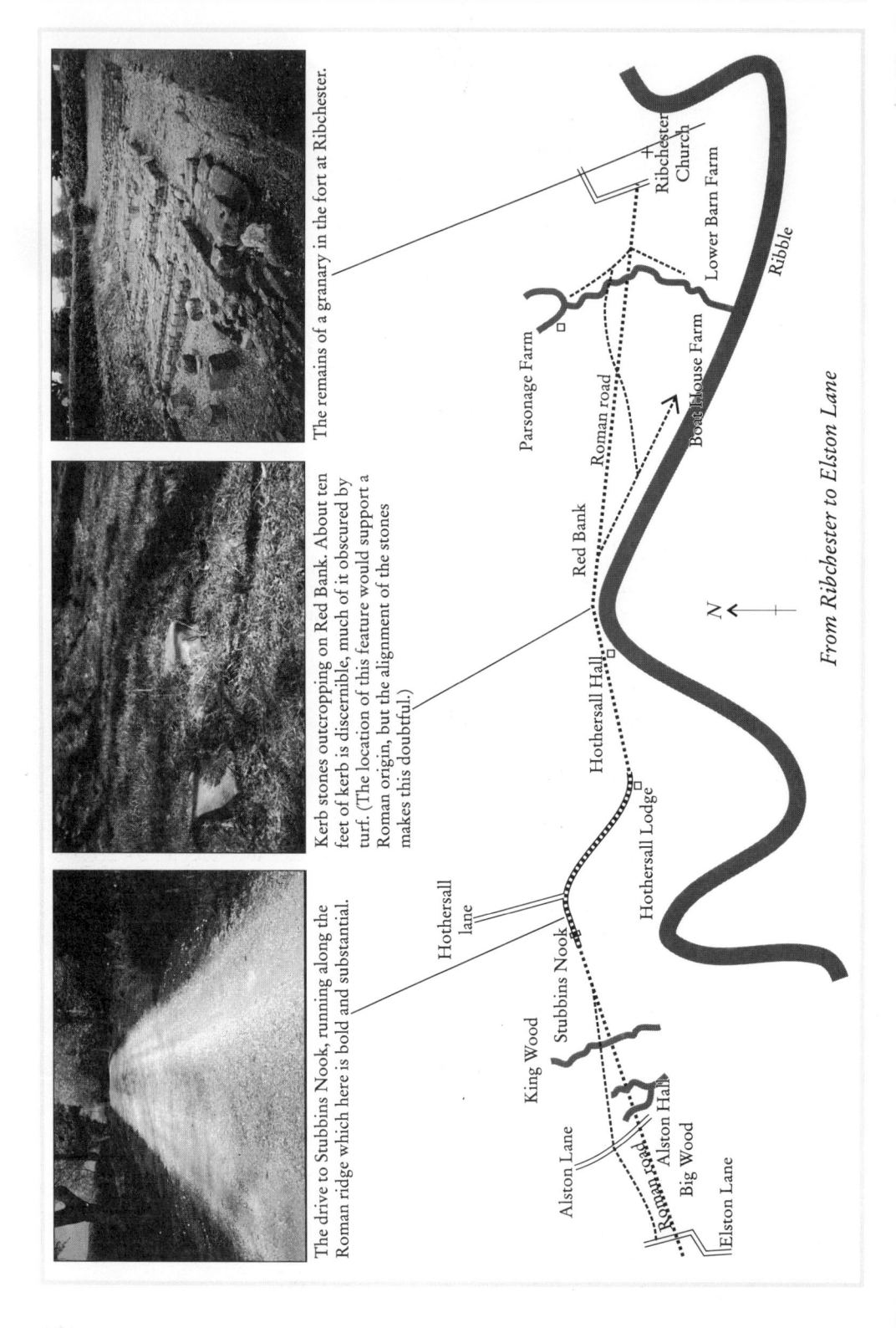

Walking Roman Roads in the Fylde and Ribble Valley

From Ribchester to Elston Lane

The drive to Stubbins Nook, running along the Roman ridge which here is bold and substantial.

Kerb stones outcropping on Red Bank. About ten feet of kerb is discernible, much of it obscured by turf. (The location of this feature would support a Roman origin, but the alignment of the stones makes this doubtful.)

The remains of a granary in the fort at Ribchester.

Part 4

The Roman Road from Ribchester to Kirkham (and beyond)

Section One
From Ribchester to Elston Lane

(Pathfinder Nos. 680, 679: Landranger No. 102)

It has generally been assumed that the first Roman northern route west of the Pennines was the military road connecting Manchester through Ribchester, Burrow in Lonsdale, and Low Borrow Bridge with Carlisle. It has been suggested (Jones, 1970) that the Roman fort at Kirkham – west of Ribchester – was a sort of outlier belonging to this same early phase, possibly to facilitate the landing of supplies at the mouth of the Ribble or Wyre. Excavations at Kirkham in 1994 suggested that Roman occupation took place mainly in the first and second centuries AD, though the picture is a complex one. Substantial traces of a road connecting Ribchester and Kirkham (and doubtless belonging to this early period) were formerly visible (Margary, 1957; Just, 1851), and indeed much evidence remains, though nowadays it is somewhat harder to find.

Excavations on the Ribchester site in 1989/90 revealed the probable course of the Kirkham road running east/west between the north wall of the fort and the vicus, or civil settlement, which grew up to the north of the fort (Buxton and Howard-Davis, 1992). In its latest phase, the road would appear to have passed some 90 metres north of the present Ribchester church. This would bring it into line with the start of the trackway to Parsonage Farm. Part of this trackway, starting about thirty yards from its eastern end, runs westwards on a pronounced ridge for perhaps 100 yards, which is then continued in direction for some distance by a hedge line. This must surely be the *agger* (Latin word for the ridge on which a Roman road was constructed) commented on by John Just in 1850. Eastwards this stretch points back to the churchyard extension, westwards it points to a clump of bushes forming a convenient marker on the hillside beyond the next field.

The modern track (with right of way) now swerves to the north towards the Parsonage farm, but in about 200 yards a footpath (still with right of way) leaves it, going west and crossing, by a substantial culvert, a stream which flows south from the direction of the Parsonage farm. About 100 yards south (downstream) of this culvert, there is a pavement of large squared flagstones in the bed of the stream which occurs nowhere else along its course. This is in line with the stretch of ridge to the east and the clump of bushes to the west mentioned above. These flagstones certainly look like the remains of an earlier paved ford; they are evidently of recent origin but perhaps indicate a former crossing point. They could not serve such a purpose now, since the banks are far too steep at this point, but the whole course of the stream has been subject to straightening, grading and embanking so that it is difficult to envisage its former aspect. John Just, writing in 1850, saw a complete section of the road exhibited in the banks of this stream, about a foot below the surface.

The footpath we have been following now swerves south again and straightens out as it passes Boat House Farm. It then swings north to follow the bend of the river – very close on its south side – and after being joined by a path from Boat House becomes quite a substantial track. It is in fact marked as a road on the first edition of the one-inch ordnance survey map, dating from the mid eighteenth century (Harley, 1970). This probably accounts for the substantial remains of metalling west of Boat house; the path itself is hardly direct enough to represent the actual Roman route. It continues to follow the first rise of the land from the river. It climbs the steep Red Bank, and from the top, having got round the river bend, it pursues an almost straight course for three quarters of a mile to Hothersall Lodge. It then turns north west and slants up a steep hillside to arrive at Stubbins Nook, where the first certainly established section of Roman road commences.

While apparently, as already indicated, too winding to represent in detail the course of the Roman road, (which hereabouts was not evident even a century ago, when copious remains of this road were visible elsewhere [Watkin, 1883]) the path we have described from the fort to Red Bank may well be quite near the line, which probably followed a straighter course a little to the north, thus keeping to the higher ground above the flood plain, as it does beyond Stubbin's Nook. Westwards from the top of Red Bank, indeed, there are sound reasons for thinking that the track is in the actual Roman line, for we have what looks like quite typical Roman planning; a straight stretch west to Hothersall Lodge, followed by a swing to the north along a short linking section, now part of Hothersall Lane, to climb, slantwise, a steep little valley side, with thereafter a resumption of the previous alignment slightly south of west, coinciding for the first two hundred yards with the drive to Stubbins Nook.

This approach driveway from Hothersall Lane to Stubbin's

Part 4

Nook, which marks the start of the line followed by the Roman road for the next four miles, runs along a quite massive *agger*, which is continued, though far less markedly, in the fields beyond. The survival of these *aggers* along minor roads, even when these are only service roads to farmhouses, is a very striking feature, probably preserved by the absence of the plough from such stretches.

As it leaves Stubbin's Nook the line of the road is flanked by two (modern) stone pillars (a feature designed to draw attention to its Roman origin ?) It is then closely followed south-westwards by the footpath marked as the Ribble Way (and by a succession of field boundaries). The actual ridge appears very distinctly, parallel to the hedge and a few yards south of it. Further west the ditch on the north side of this ridge, alongside the hedge, appears to have become a stream feeding into the brook which eventually flows from north to south across the line of the road (the brook is not named on the Pathfinder map but is shown flowing south from King Wood to the Ribble).

As the modern Ribble Way approaches this brook it swings to the north along the edge of the wood which here forms the northern boundary of the field, to cross the stream by a footbridge. But the Roman line can be seen going straight on and then veering left (south) to enter a smoothly graded cutting by which it descends the bank of the quite deep gorge through which the brook flows. The cutting is flanked on each side by substantial ridges – possibly formed by the material excavated in digging it. On the west side of the stream another, less evident, cutting slants up to continue the line.

Continuing westwards, the Roman line soon crosses the lane leading north to Jinkinson's Farm (the footpath marking the Ribble Way is now a short distance to the north, roughly parallel but still

The cutting descending to the east bank of the stream which flows south from King Wood across the course of the road. This photograph was taken from the top of the cutting, looking west towards the stream, which is marked by the trees.

The cutting and embankment at the crossing of the stream east of Alston Hall.

Looking east up the cutting by which the road emerges from Big Wood, east of Elston Lane.

diverging). The Roman road is marked by a hedge to the next north-south stream, again flowing through a fairly deep gorge. Once again a clearly defined cutting – this time much steeper – descends to the stream, and on the western bank are the damaged remains of what could be a slanting terrace climbing the bank. The line of the road continues to point south-west, heading for Alston Hall, which can be seen through the trees, but traces are difficult to find, except again at the next stream crossing, where the cuttings marking the approach from each side are again evident. A hundred years ago remains of the road in this area were much more visible; ploughing frequently revealed the metalling. (Watkin, 1883).

The line now crosses Alston Lane and enters the grounds of Alston Hall – where its surface was noted during the construction of the new Observatory (Olivier, 1978) – at this point it is some three hundred yards south of the Ribble Way. Beyond the Hall a field boundary follows it for a short distance, but there is little other sign. Traces are however found south of Marsh House, where the road descends what appears to be quite a massive cutting to enter a very overgrown wood – the northern end of Big Wood shown on Pathfinder 679. It passes a deep ravine on its northern side and emerges by another cutting into the field east of Elston Lane. It then crosses this field, close to the northern edge, and finally crosses the lane itself, our termination for this section.

Note on access. In Ribchester, the (free) car park is conveniently situated close to the Roman museum and the remains of the fort baths (both of which the visitor will want to inspect); it is also adjacent to the start of the footpath followed in this chapter. There is right of way throughout the whole length of this path (or series of paths/roads) from Ribchester to Stubbin's Nook, though, as is evident from the text, this succession of paths indicates rather the general direction than the exact route of the Roman road. From Stubbins Nook the Ribble Way (again with right of way) follows the Roman line – now more certainly established – almost to the point where the brook flowing from King Wood is reached, after which the Ribble way diverges to the north, but remains near enough, all the way to Alston Lane, for observation to be continued. Thereafter the grounds of Alston Hall intervene; indeed the Hall buildings stand squarely upon the line, thus effectively barring investigation for some considerable distance.

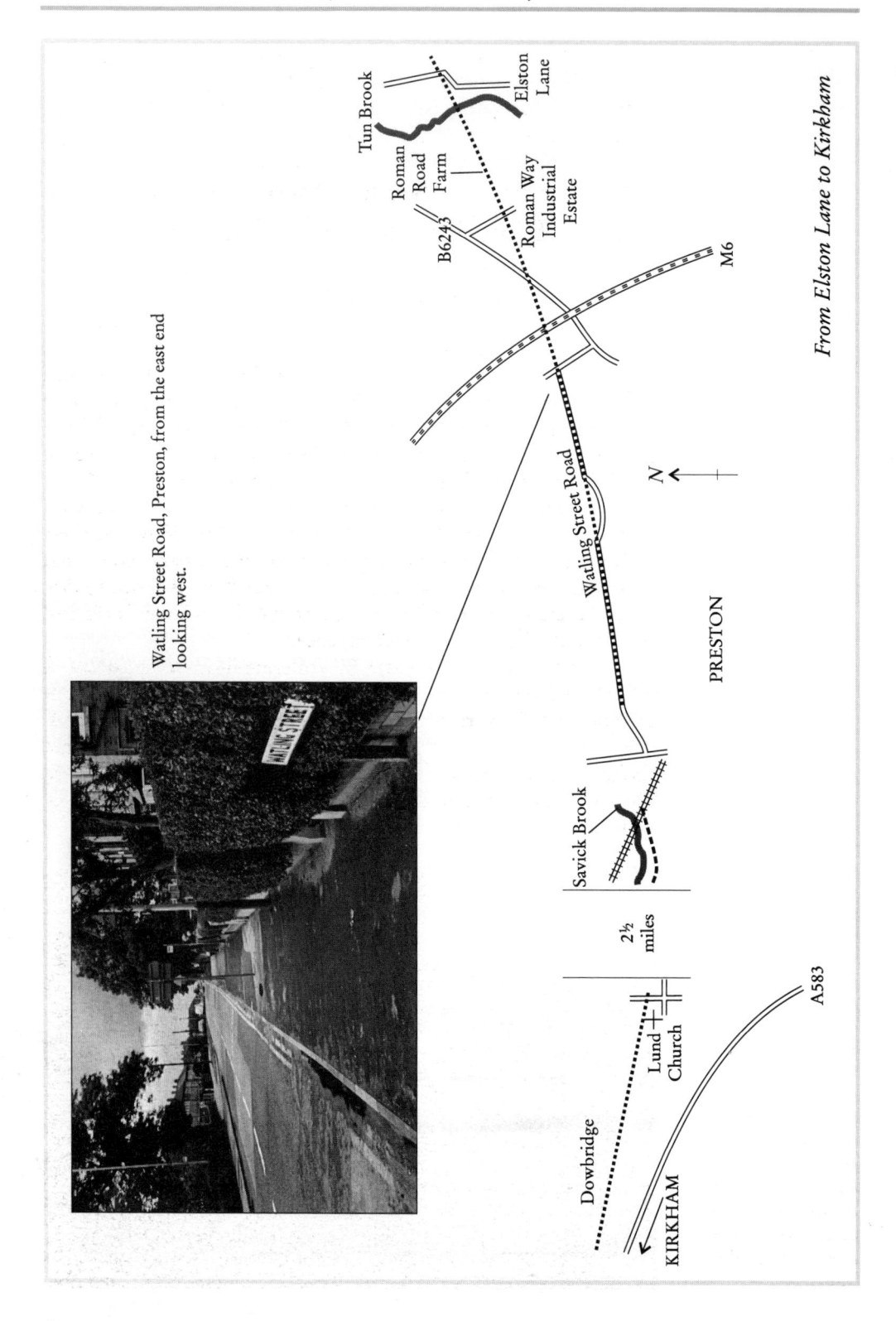

Walking Roman Roads in the Fylde and Ribble Valley

Tun Brook
Elston Lane
Roman Road Farm
B6243
Roman Way Industrial Estate
M6
Watling Street Road
N
PRESTON
Savick Brook
2½ miles
Dowbridge
Lund Church
A583
KIRKHAM

From Elston Lane to Kirkham

Watling Street Road, Preston, from the east end looking west.

60

Section Two
From Elston Lane to Kirkham

(Pathfinder 679: Landranger 102)

WEST of the drive leading from Elston Lane to the house called the Bungalow, the line of the Roman road is very plain indeed as it crosses the field to Tun Brook Wood. It is marked by a pronounced ditch, with remains of a line of trees, and with traces of the ridge as the brook is approached. The steep banks of Tun Brook are so covered with woods and undergrowth that it is very difficult to discern the course of the road across the valley. However there are signs of a curving terraceway on the steep east bank, going first north and then south. The course on the west bank is obscure, after which access becomes difficult until Roman Road Farm is reached and the outskirts of Preston commence.

The section which follows, while offering little to the walker, is full of interest for the genuine enthusiast. It provides a prime example of Roman road survival in urban and semi-urban environment, giving signs of its presence in various ways – in very slight surface traces, in an assortment of names on the map, some ancient and some modern, but above all in a couple of miles of straight, undeviating city street.

The ridge and ditch crossing the field east of Tun Brook, which is marked by the trees in the distance (the withered tree stands on the ridge).

The first examples of place names are soon met with. Roman Road Farm, about three-fifths of a mile south-west of Tun Brook along the line of the road, heads the list. Just to the west of Roman Road Farm the industrial estate, shown on Pathfinder Map 679, is called, significantly enough, Roman Way Estate. The main access road to this estate from B 6243 forms, after a short distance, the western boundary of the field between the farm and the estate. Looking eastwards across this field the line of the Roman road is clearly discernible by humps in the near (western) fence and in the far (north-eastern) corner. It points directly to Roman Road Farm, clearly visible across the field. In the driveway to the Crematorium which borders the west side of the Roman Way Estate, the line seems to be marked by gaps in the hedges on the eastern side of the drive, but no trace is visible in the rough ground to the west. A factory block now intervenes, and there are no further signs westwards until the built-up area of Preston is reached on the other side of the M 6.

Here the Roman line is soon taken up again, first by a length of pathway, about 150 yards in extent, giving access to a school, and then, on the same alignment, by Watling Street Road which runs dead straight for about three quarters of a mile. The name Watling Street clearly survives from before the expansion of Preston, when the road was crossing the open country known as Fulwood Moor. (Watkin, 1883).

The true Roman line seems to be followed by the south pavement of Watling Street Road and to be marked by an overgrown hedge in front of Brookfield Methodist Church at the eastern end of the street. This is hardly likely to be a survival of the *agger* but may well be a stretch of boundary bank following the old road. Continuing the route westwards, we reach the point where Watling Street Road swerves south to avoid the site of Fulwood Barracks. Beyond this point the line appears to be continued for a short distance by a distinct hump in the gardens on the opposite side of East Way. After about three quarters of a mile, beyond the site of Fulwood Barracks, Watling Street Road again comes on to the Roman line, with a slight change of alignment towards the north. This time the line is again followed rigidly westwards to the crossing of the Garstang road, and after that by the Lytham Road as far as the railway, making a total of over a mile. Beyond this a minor road follows the line almost to Haslam Park.

Actual traces of the road are virtually absent from now on. However a straight stretch of footpath south of the Savick Brook is almost on the line which we have been following. Just north of a school marked on Pathfinder 679, this path bends briefly to the north on a course which, if continued, would point just north of west to the line through Lea, Salwick, Lund and Dowbridge along which earlier writers saw very distinct traces of the road which now seem to have disappeared. In 1851 this road was described as 'most perfect' in the vicinity of Lea (Thornber, 1851). Further west, just beyond the large area of works west of Salwick, Margary saw traces of the ridge in the fields near Lund Church (which Margary calls Clifton Church), but I have never been able to make these out. Moreover there is mention in a charter of 1190 of a 'great street stretching from Dowbridge to Lund' and around 1300 a field near Dowbridge is called 'Watlingstreet' (France, 1945) so it would appear that the road ran from Lund church to Dowbridge on the outskirts of Kirkham. In the fields west of New Hey lane (which runs north from Newton) I have seen traces of an east-west ridge which may represent the line.

Note on access. The actual crossing of Tun Brook is not accessible to the public, but the approach to it from the east is visible from the drive to 'The Bungalow'. The faint but interesting traces of the road between Roman Road farm and Roman Way Industrial Estate can be seen from the access road to the estate. Watlingstreet Road through the Fulwood district of Preston can, of course, be walked or driven and is an interesting example of the survival of a Roman line in urban surroundings. Westwards towards Kirkham traces are hard to find; the footpath south of Savick Brook which may represent the line is accessible, and from Lund Church the reader might like to view the adjacent fields in the hope of detecting the ridge which was earlier visible.

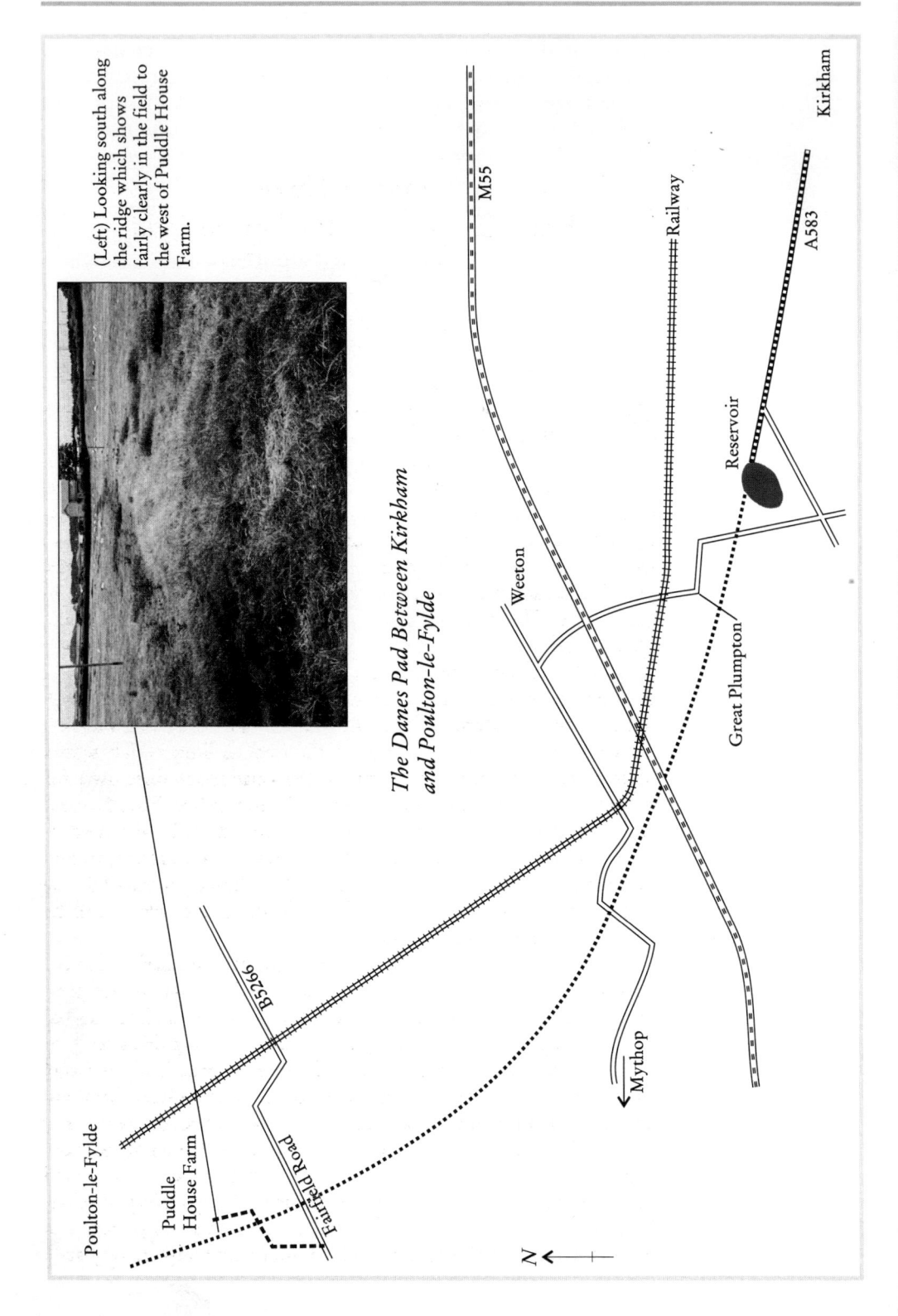

Walking Roman Roads in the Fylde and Ribble Valley

(Left) Looking south along the ridge which shows fairly clearly in the field to the west of Puddle House Farm.

The Danes Pad Between Kirkham and Poulton-le-Fylde

Section Three
From Kirkham to Poulton-le-Fylde
(The Dane's Pad)

(Pathfinder 679, 678: Landranger 102)

At Kirkham, the immediate destination of the road we have been following, a military base was established on Carr Hill, probably early in the Roman period (though its military character, on present evidence, was apparently short-lived [Shotter, 1993]). However there is a considerable body of opinion to support the continuation of the road west of Kirkham, heading for a port on the coast. In this area the road beyond Kirkham was locally known as the Dane's Pad, and was much described by earlier antiquaries (e.g. John Just and W. Thornber in 1850. Thornber was of the opinion that the Danes made use of the road to penetrate inland when raiding the district; hence the name). It was accepted as Roman by Margary and is shown on the O.S. map of Roman Britain (1991 edition), though with a marked difference. The O.S. map of Roman Britain shows it as two straight alignments, not in the broken lines which would indicate an uncertain course, but in the continuous lines used for roads where the course has been definitely established. But Margary, and indeed most if not all his predecessors, describe the road as tracing a smooth curve across the Fylde – a very unusual path to find in a Roman road. This, indeed is how it is shown on the O.S. one inch map (Landranger 102), and this is the route which will be followed in the account below.

Margary, writing nearly forty years ago, was emphatic that very little remained above ground in his day, and I must confess that, despite diligent search, I have found few traces of the Dane's Pad, and certainly nothing that will justify recommending this stretch to the interested walker, for whom this book is principally written. This may be partly due to limited access; once away from Kirkham and the A 583 the line keeps very clear of modern roads. This is not unusual in a Roman road, but enthusiasts must have noticed how often a Roman route is still followed by a right of way, even when this is now simply a succession of stiles or field gates. No part of the Dane's Pad seems to have survived as a route in this way, and instances of its ever being crossed by a public footpath are very rare;

indeed the path from Todderstaffe Hall to Staining is, to the best of my knowledge, one of the very few examples. Nevertheless, for the sake of completeness, I shall set out the few indications which I have found along the route of the Dane's Pad sketched out on the map, in the hope that others, more fortunate in gaining access (or more perceptive in observation) might add to the rather meagre list.

Starting at Kirkham and travelling westwards, we first note the straight stretch of the A 583, continued, when the main road bends to the south at Whinbrick, by the lane to the reservoir, giving a total alignment of about a mile; this is generally accepted as following the first section of the Dane's Pad. For the next sign – not very pronounced – we need to go on to Great Plumpton village, where a ridge may be seen in the field north of Oakfield farm, heading north-west towards the disused railway (Pathfinder no 678 covers this and the following locations). This presumably is the ridge noted by Margary (p 107), who wrote when the railway was still in use, a point which might well confuse the later enquirer.

Further along the line (following the curved route shown on the Landranger map, since this seems to have the weight of opinion in its favour) the minor road eastwards from Mythop to Weeton makes a sharp bend from N E to S E not far west of the (Blackpool) railway (not the disused line mentioned above). Immediately to the east of this bend a scatter of stones is visible in the field to the south of the road under suitable conditions, i.e. when the field has recently been ploughed, and traces of a ridge appear on the same line, going north-west, on the north side of the road.

I found the most interesting signs of the Dane's Pad, and they are not exactly spectacular, in the vicinity of Puddle House Farm, to the north-east of Hardhorn village, just south of Poulton-le-Fylde. The approach lane to the farm from B 5266 bends sharply to the east and then sharply to the north before reaching the farm buildings (see Pathfinder 678). The line of Dane's Pad crosses the east-west section of this lane and heads north across the field (Margary, 1957), passing just west of the farm buildings. It shows as a damaged ridge, quite plainly at the north end of the field, marked here by a couple of tree stumps and elsewhere by clumps of nettles. Very likely a hedge formerly followed the line. Incidentally, earlier documents show the name of the farm as Paddle House, which might well derive from the name Dane's Pad. (Pad is evidently a local dialect form of path or road). North of the farm buildings I could find no signs, and indeed this is the point to which the Dane's Pad was traced by earlier writers. It was thought to be heading for a harbour on the Wyre estuary, and there has been speculation that this might have been *Portus Setantiorum*, the Roman port mentioned by Ptolemy of Alexandria in the second century AD and located by him in north-west Britain. Indeed there seems to be some evidence to connect this elusive Roman harbour with the Fleetwood area (Shotter and White,

1995), which would fit in quite well with the direction of the Dane's Pad as observed near Puddle House.

As noted above, this road was much talked of by earlier antiquaries. Even along the road leading west from Kirkham (now the A 583 and doubtless very much changed) we are told that 'numerous Roman remains may be detected' in walking along the verges, though without details as to their exact nature. The writer is John Just who in 1851 also observes that further west an 'immense embankment, several yards in height' traversed the low ground, and refers to 'frequent sections of the road' in the drainage channels which often crossed it. W. Thornber, in the same year, writes of a mound, 'twelve yards broad at the crown, and twenty yards broad at the base'. It certainly seems to have been a landmark locally. However, both writers mention that it was used as a source of gravel by local farmers, and perhaps this accounts for its being so less conspicuous nowadays.

Note on access. Difficulty of access has already been noted in the text above. For the first mile or so from Kirkham the A 583 has obliterated all traces except the line itself, and where this road bends at Whinbrick the lane onwards to the reservoir (thought to continue the Roman line) was not open at my last visit. The only other points of public access are the minor road from Weeton to Mythop, the footpath from Todderstaffe Hall to Staining, and the road south of Puddle House Farm leading to Hardhorn. John Just's account – written of course nearly 150 years ago – seems to indicate the low-lying area between Hardhorn in the north and Mythop Hall in the south as the district in which the Dane's Pad was to be seen in its greatest strength. I have explored a good deal of the north and south parts of this expanse, besides walking across the central ground on the Todderstaffe/Staining track, without finding any very obvious remains.

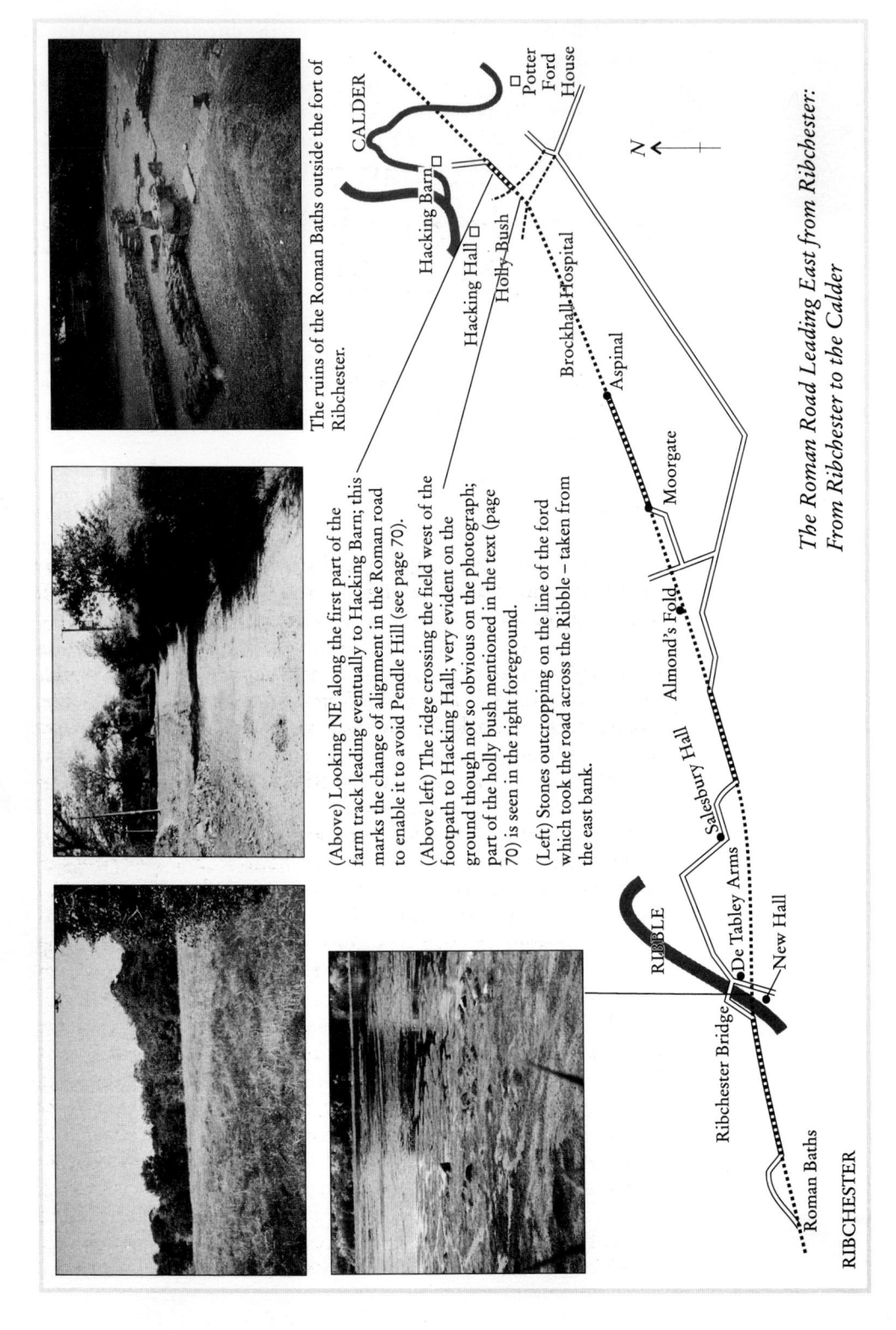

Walking Roman Roads in the Fylde and Ribble Valley

The ruins of the Roman Baths outside the fort of Ribchester.

(Above) Looking NE along the first part of the farm track leading eventually to Hacking Barn; this marks the change of alignment in the Roman road to enable it to avoid Pendle Hill (see page 70).

(Above left) The ridge crossing the field west of the footpath to Hacking Hall; very evident on the ground though not so obvious on the photograph; part of the holly bush mentioned in the text (page 70) is seen in the right foreground.

(Left) Stones outcropping on the line of the ford which took the road across the Ribble – taken from the east bank.

The Roman Road Leading East from Ribchester: From Ribchester to the Calder

68

Part 5

The Roman road leading eastwards from Ribchester along the Ribble Valley

Section One
From Ribchester to the Calder

(Pathfinder no. 680: Landranger no. 103)

THE road eastward along the Ribble valley, leading to the fort at Elslack and then on through the Aire Gap, is probably the most interesting of all those leaving Ribchester (always excepting the Bowland section of the main north/south road, described in an earlier volume). It was important as being one of the trans-Pennine routes surveyed and used by the Romans; its ultimate destination at its eastern end is York. Thus it links the two main roads to the north on each side of the Pennines. We follow it in this volume as far as Downham – i.e. until it leaves the Ribble valley, where it has left definite and very interesting traces.

A good starting point for investigating the road (after a visit to the museum if this has not already been seen) would be the ruins of the bath-house, not far to the north-east of the fort. The course of the road is just to the south of these, crossing the field in a north-easterly direction immediately north of the river, and then falling into the course of the Blackburn road where this straightens out on its approach to Little Town. There are now no visible remains of this stretch. Where the Blackburn road turns towards the north along the river bank to approach the bridge, the Roman road continued on its course, and all indications are that it forded the river at this point. This would bring it to the opposite bank of the Ribble at a point between New Hall and the De Tabley Arms. Looking back from here the line of the ford is indicated by the large amount of stone on the river bed, projecting above the stream when the river is low, and causing broken water when it is in spate. Just north of New Hall the east bank itself appears to have been cut away to form a hollow way by which the road left the river on its eastward course, but on my recent visits this has been so choked with undergrowth that investigation has been difficult.

The O.S. Pathfinder map no. 680 shows the course of the Roman road passing just north of New Hall in a direction slightly north of east, which in about two thirds of a mile brings it to a point south of Salesbury Hall, but I have been unable to find any traces along this low-lying stretch. Near Salesbury Hall the line leaves the Ribble flood plain, and appears to be marked as a terrace on the hillside seen to the south of the present (Ribchester/Langho) road as this skirts the wood south-east of the Hall. For a short distance it then merges with the present road, and with it makes a slight change of alignment more to the north; in typically Roman fashion this occurs on a hilltop with wide views around. Shortly afterwards the modern road swings south but the Roman line continues straight on, marked by a stretch of ridge which is shown on the Pathfinder map, though the field containing it is not readily accessible. However the line continues straight ahead for the next mile, passing beneath three sets of farm buildings – Almond's Fold, Moorgate and Aspinalls. Between Moorgate and Aspinalls it is accompanied by a farm track (with right of way), and this has the quite wide verges which frequently occur on old lengths of road.

East of Aspinalls the line continues to be marked by field boundaries as it descends quite steeply to Dinkley Brook, beyond which it enters the grounds of Brockhall Hospital. Before the hospital was built the ridge was traceable in this area (Codrington 1918). Nowadays it is not evident until the vicinity of Hacking Hall is reached, about half a mile beyond the eastern hospital boundary. Here convenient access is afforded by the footpath which leads left (north westwards) from the approach lane to Potter Ford House, just after this lane has left the Old Langho road (the Pathfinder 680 map is indispensable here, as elsewhere; the footpath is the right-hand one of the two shown as forking from near this point). About 200 yards along the footpath a holly bush in the hedge on the left (west) marks the crossing point of the Roman line. It is worth an effort to locate this point, since the situation just here is interesting.

Standing near this holly bush and looking south- westwards across the field, i.e. in the direction opposite to that of the photograph on page 71, the Roman ridge, with side ditches, can be made out quite clearly, crossing the field and pointing – in a north-easterly direction – to the great mass of Pendle Hill. At this precise point, or very near it, the Roman road makes quite a pronounced change of direction, more to the north, and by standing with one's back to the bush, the start of this new alignment can be made out, marked for the first short distance by a farm track (which later turns off north to Hacking Barn). This is a particularly interesting change of direction since it was obviously made to avoid Pendle Hill, clearly visible ahead. This new alignment, which is followed for the next six miles

Part 5

Looking north-east along the Roman road (coming from the direction of Brockhall Hospital) as it approaches the change of alignment point marked by the holly bush mentioned in the text. The ridge and ditches can just be made out (they are far clearer on the ground); the holly bush stands alone on the line, the track marking the new direction is seen behind it, and in the distance is seen (hazily) the mass of Pendle Hill, which caused the change.

i.e. until this formidable obstacle has been passed, brings our road, in rather less than half a mile, to the River Calder and to the end of this section.

Note on access. There is free and open admission to the bath-house at Ribchester; the site of the ford over the Ribble can be viewed from Ribchester Bridge or from the south bank of the river. Between Moorgate Farm and Aspinall's the line is followed by a footpath with right of way, and the same is true for a short distance east of Brockhall Hospital. A public footpath, with right of way, gives access to the point near Hacking Hall where the highly interesting change of alignment, described in the text, may be studied. There is no public access onwards to the Calder crossing.

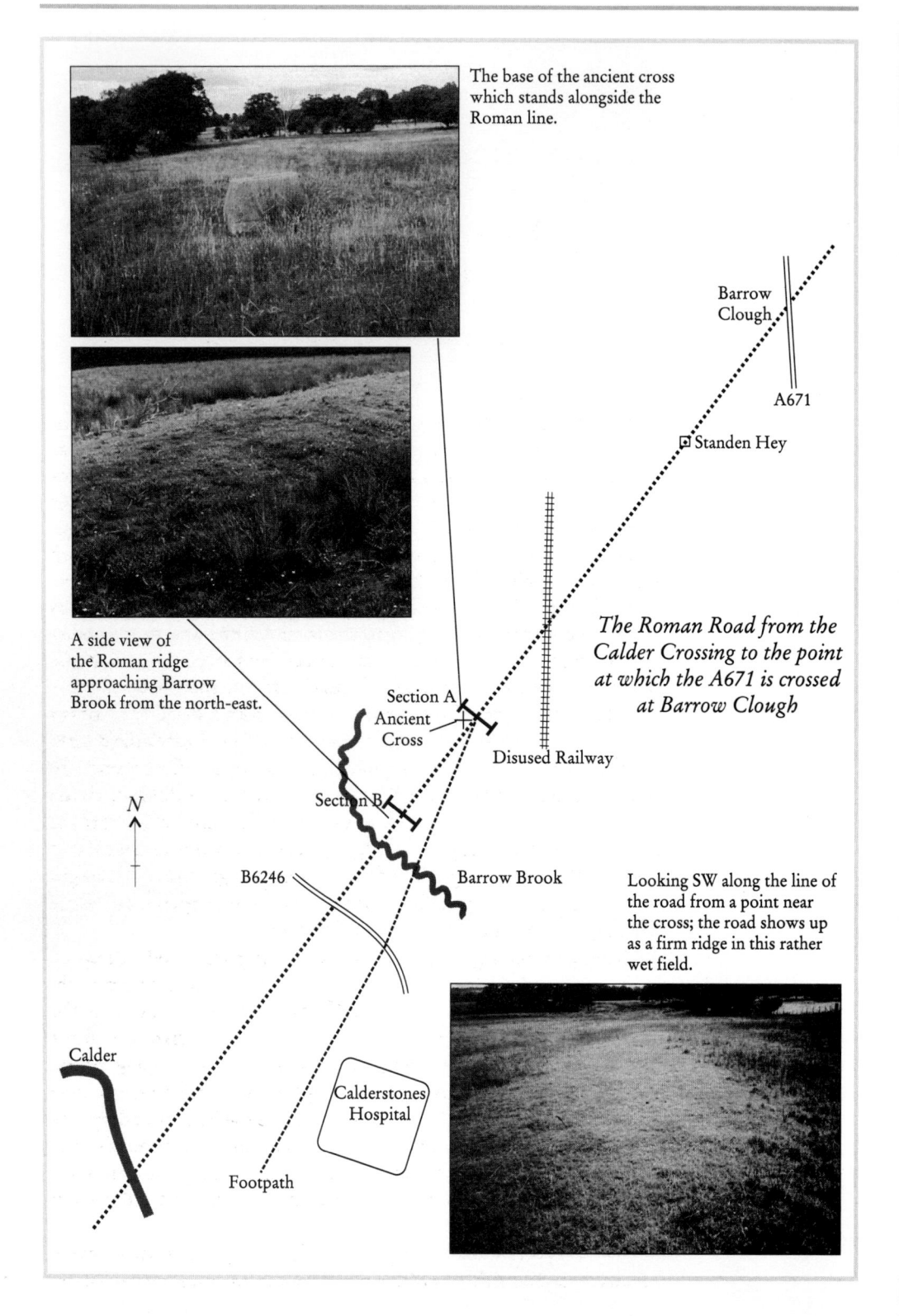

Walking Roman Roads in the Fylde and Ribble Valley

The base of the ancient cross which stands alongside the Roman line.

A side view of the Roman ridge approaching Barrow Brook from the north-east.

Barrow Clough

A671

Standen Hey

Section A
Ancient Cross

Disused Railway

Section B

The Roman Road from the Calder Crossing to the point at which the A671 is crossed at Barrow Clough

N

B6246

Barrow Brook

Looking SW along the line of the road from a point near the cross; the road shows up as a firm ridge in this rather wet field.

Calder

Calderstones Hospital

Footpath

72

Part 5

Section Two
From the Calder to the A671
at Barrow Clough

(Pathfinder 680: Landranger 103)

THE change of direction described in the last section brings the road on to a bearing which is practically north-east, and as already recorded, the alignment now commenced is rigidly maintained for the next six miles. Throughout almost the whole of this distance the road is marked by features of some kind – by hedgerows, paths or tracks, and when free of these, by the *agger* on which it is built and which is often prominent. All in all, this is a remarkable survival in a relatively low-lying, mostly arable countryside. It is regrettable that towards the end of this stretch the new A 59 Clitheroe by-pass has obliterated some traces, and one hopes that the remainder of this fine stretch will survive future road building.

After crossing the Calder and emerging from a wood the Roman line is followed closely by field boundaries until it crosses the B 6246 Whalley/Mitton road about three- quarters of a mile beyond the river. Almost parallel to the Roman line, but a short distance to the south-east, is an old footpath leading originally from Potter Ford on the Calder (and, on my last visit, signposted, when it crosses the B 6246, to Barrow Clough Wood). This footpath gradually converges to the Roman line until, about one third of a mile north-east of the Whalley/Mitton road, the two finally merge.

Being a public right of way, this footpath gives excellent opportunities of studying the Roman road in a most interesting stretch. The two are perhaps two hundred yards apart when they cross the B 6246, and still closer when they meet Barrow Brook a short distance further on. The footpath crosses this by stepping stones (quite tricky when the stream is flowing strongly) and on the far side of the brook, a little to the north-west beside the field boundary, the ridge of the Roman road can be seen in considerable strength. It is very noticeable that in the vicinity of stream crossings Roman roads are often much raised; perhaps this was to cope with wet and marshy ground.

The footpath finally merges with the Roman line about three hundred yards north east of Barrow Brook, and continues to follow

Section A
Taken near ancient cross

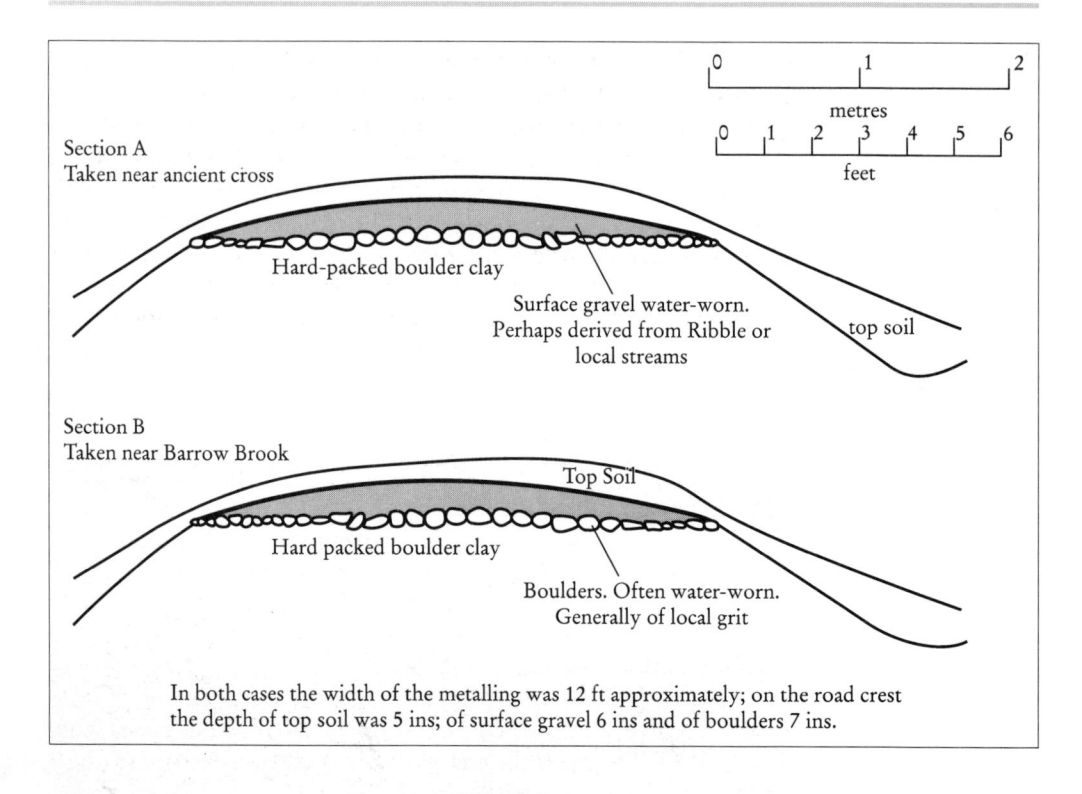

Hard-packed boulder clay

Surface gravel water-worn. Perhaps derived from Ribble or local streams

top soil

Section B
Taken near Barrow Brook

Top Soil

Hard packed boulder clay

Boulders. Often water-worn. Generally of local grit

In both cases the width of the metalling was 12 ft approximately; on the road crest the depth of top soil was 5 ins; of surface gravel 6 ins and of boulders 7 ins.

Above: Sections taken across the Roman road in the field north-east of Barrow Brook.

Left: The stone referred to in the text as a possible milestone; it was found half-buried near Barrow Brook.

it, with right of way, for more than a mile. Until the (disused) Blackburn/Clitheroe railway is reached, the route traverses rough pasture, which has probably seldom, or never, been ploughed, and consequently remains of the road are unusually plentiful. The ridge is often prominent and the line is marked by difference of vegetation and quite frequent outcrops of metalling. A parish boundary follows the hedge which accompanies the Roman road for half a mile beyond (north east) of Barrow Brook, and it is probably this which accounts for the old cross, the base of which still stands boldly alongside the road at a point where the ridge is especially evident.

Here a personal note may perhaps be excused. Almost forty years ago, when I was a headmaster in Blackburn, I asked permission to cut two sections across the line of the Roman road in this field. As mentioned in the foreword, the necessary authorisation was readily given by Mr E. Holgate, of Standen Hey farm, who indeed took great interest in the project. So for the next few weeks, with the enthusiastic help of parties of schoolboys, the road was excavated at two points – firstly near the old cross (where the modern footpath follows the road) and secondly to the south-west near the crossing of Barrow Brook, where the road is quite derelict. The results of course were fully recorded and are shown opposite. In both instances the road was revealed in a good state of preservation, with both the foundation layer of large boulders and the surface layer of gravel present. The substantial construction of this stretch was no

Looking north-east along the substantial ridge from about 200 yards south-west of the old cross.

The sections shown opposite indicate that the Roman road has survived practically intact in this area. Hence it is not surprising to see the metalling frequently outcropping, as in the example shown here.

doubt in response to the heavy clay subsoil and the consequent wet surface. The width of the metalling was about twelve feet.

The stone shown in the photograph on page 74 was found – half-buried – alongside the road at a point in the vicinity of section B, i.e. by a derelict stretch. It was evidently originally cylindrical in shape, though greatly mutilated; the diameter would be about twelve inches and the surviving length about thirty inches. There was no trace of any inscription, but the shape and position of the stone give some ground for regarding it as possibly a damaged Roman milestone. This was indeed the opinion of Mr. Ivan D. Margary, to whom were sent copies of the photographs and of the report on the sections excavated, and whose favourable comments were much valued by the author.

After crossing the (now disused) Blackburn/Clitheroe railway line, the Roman road becomes an enclosed overgrown track, still pursuing its very straight north-eastern alignment. On the approach to the farm buildings of Standen Hey, which stand on it, the road was being roughly surfaced on my last visit. Previously the metalling was frequently visible in this stretch; it can still be detected in a fenced-off strip on the eastern side of the road. The right-of-way goes through the farmyard and continues on the Roman line, which is now followed by the farm access road to the A671. The outcropping metalling was formerly a feature of this length also, but it is now smoothly surfaced and maintained; the only relic of its Roman origin (besides its straightness) is the pronounced ridge on which it runs.

About eighty yards before the A671 is reached, the farm road swerves to the right (south) but the Roman ridge continues straight on to the main road, showing strongly despite being somewhat masked by the thick growth of trees which stand upon it – an unusual survival worth noting.

Looking north-east along the agger described in the text, which lies under the trees alongside the north-eastern end of the drive (seen on the right) from Standen Hey to the A671 (see in the background through the trees).

Note on access. From Barrow Brook to Standen Hey Farm, this highly interesting stretch of Roman road can be followed by using the path, with right of way, which initially runs close by and a little to the south of it and later coincides with it. This is very fortunate for the Roman road enthusiast, since this is a stretch which should certainly not be missed. As indicated above, the right of way continues through the farmyard and then follows the drive leading to the A671, giving one the opportunity to study the agger under the trees on one's left as the main road is reached.

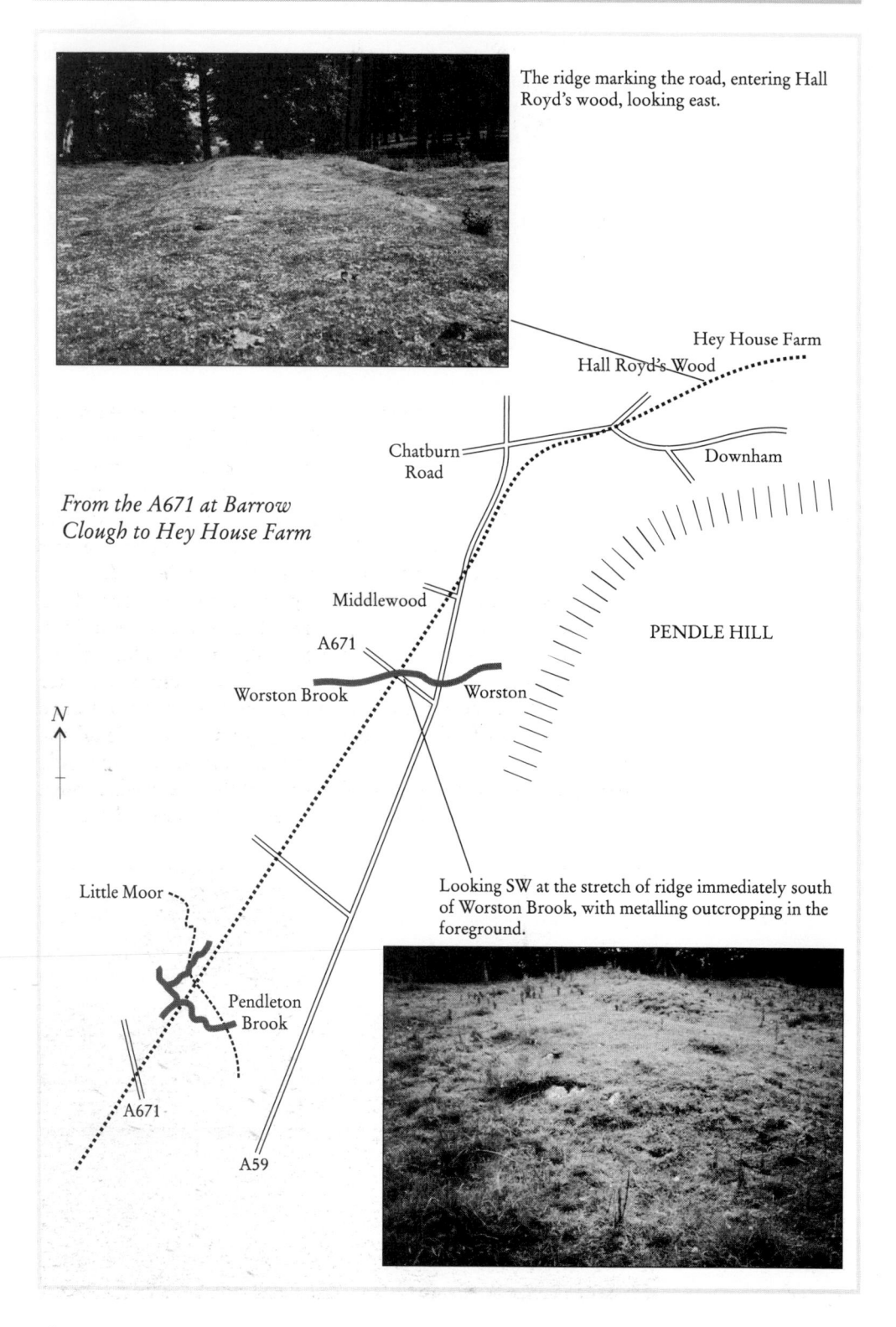

Walking Roman Roads in the Fylde and Ribble Valley

The ridge marking the road, entering Hall Royd's wood, looking east.

From the A671 at Barrow Clough to Hey House Farm

Looking SW at the stretch of ridge immediately south of Worston Brook, with metalling outcropping in the foreground.

Part 5

Section Three
From the A671 at Barrow Clough to Hey House Farm

(Pathfinder 669: Landranger 103)

For 3½ miles after crossing the A671, the Roman line shows up with remarkable clarity on the Pathfinder Map (no. 669) as a succession of field boundaries and paths. There is, unfortunately, no right of way along any part of it, but it is occasionally crossed by public paths which enable some stretches to be investigated. One such stretch – and a very interesting one – is crossed by the path (with right of way) leading from Little Moor to Pendleton. Just after the path has crossed the first footbridge after leaving Little Moor, the Roman ridge is seen traversing the field in great strength from south-west to north-east, marked for some distance by a line of trees and with its eastern ditch especially prominent. Where the track from Little Moor crosses it the metalling can be seen in places, and south-westwards of this the ridge is very prominent as Pendleton Brook is approached. It swerves to the west somewhat, apparently to avoid the junction point of a tributary, and then descends to what has obviously been a ford, with much stone in the stream bed.

Looking north-east along the ridge as it approaches Pendleton Brook.

The ford across Pendleton Brook, viewed from the north bank.

    Shortly afterwards the outskirts of Clitheroe intervene for a short distance, but the road reenters open country beyond and continues as a rigidly straight line of hedges with parish boundaries following it north of High Moor and again north of Worston. Just beyond the point where it is again crossed by the A671, a short distance west of Worston, the Roman road crosses Worston Brook; this point is accessible by footpath and is well worth visiting. The ancient hedge marking the line on both sides of the stream is very clear, but it stops short on the south side and in the gap remains of the ridge are visible, with stones outcropping here and there. In the north bank of the brook a section of metalling is exposed.

    North of Middlewood a track formerly followed the line, but after a few yards this is now obliterated by the new A59 – the Clitheroe by-pass – which, unfortunately, either covers or cuts off access to the Roman road for the next mile. However, just before the Chatburn road is carried over the A59 (traffic seeking it must turn off earlier) the Roman line turns off to the east, resuming its general alignment, since it can now pass round the north end of Pendle Hill. This turn takes it on a course just south of the road to Chatburn, though not quite parallel to it. In fact the Roman road gradually approaches the modern road, showing as a ridge in the grounds of Downham Hall, just over the boundary wall.

    Finally the Roman line and the Chatburn road merge for the last few yards before the latter forks at the turn-off to Downham. The Roman road continues straight on at the fork, in a direction just north of east, and passes through a wood, from which it emerges as a swelling in the ground, low but quite distinct, running along the top of a ridge to the north of Downham, with splendid views of Pendle Hill to the south. In a quarter of a mile it reaches Hall Royds

Part 5

Looking south from near Worston Brook along the old hedge marking the Roman road as it approaches the brook from the south-west.

Looking north-east along the line of trees marking the road north of the brook; in the foreground the metalling clearly shows in the bank.

Looking west along the stretch of *agger* just inside (south of) the wall of Downham Hall grounds, very near the main gate.

Looking south across the ridge, which shows up as a level line against the background of Pendle Hill.

Wood, where metalling appears round the trees which stand on or near it. East of the wood the ridge is bold and prominent for a short distance, until the line is taken up by the lane leading to Hey House Farm.

Traces of this road continue to be evident on its journey east to the fort at Elslack (and beyond that to Ilkley), but we have reached the point at which it leaves the Ribble valley (and incidentally Pathfinder 669); this then is an appropriate place to conclude our investigation.

Note on access. As noted in the text, paths with right of way cross the line at various points as it skirts Clitheroe. The Little Moor/Pendleton path gives access to the interesting section north east of Pendleton Brook, and public tracks on both sides of the A671 enable investigation of the equally interesting crossing of Worston Brook. Further on the A59 now effectively masks the stretch which runs past Worsaw Hill, but the ridge is visible from the Chatburn road, just inside Downham Hall Park. A footpath from Downham village gives access to the Roman road as it emerges from the wood east of the Chatburn road fork, and at the eastern end of the same field a path from Twiston Lane with right of way, makes possible investigation of the area around Hall Royd Wood.

Appendix

Finds of Roman material on or near the routes followed in this volume

As one might expect, various Roman items (mostly coins) have come to light in the vicinity of these roads, quite often by accident. I must confess that (like many another enthusiast) I live in hopes of similar chance discoveries; so far I have been rewarded by the possible milestone mentioned on page 74, and considered authentic enough to be recorded in a reputable archaeological journal. For most of the information in this appendix – especially that about coins – I am indebted once again to Dr David Shotter, and I refer the interested reader to his recent publications (Shotter, 1990, 1995). It should be stressed, however, that in the majority of cases, again especially for coins, details of precise find-spots are not available; hence the frequent approximations in the following paragraphs.

Taking the Ribchester/Lancaster road first, a coin of Nerva (96–98 AD) was recorded in the Dilworth area, near Written Stone farm; this presumably was the coin seen and described by S. Jackson at the farm – it was found by a boy digging a drain alongside the road (Jackson, 1897). Much further on, near Dolphinholme on the approach to Galgate, fourth-century coins of Helena and Constans were discovered. In the same area, near the Wyre crossing, an erstwhile resident of the district remembers, in the 1960s, a metalled surface being uncovered during gravel extraction; nearby an inscribed stone came to light which by its size and shape could well have been a Roman milestone.

The sculptures unearthed at Burrow Heights, alongside the Preston/Lancaster road, have been described in the main text; from the same site came coins of Hadrian (117–138 AD) and Claudius 11 (268–270 AD). Further south along this same route, in the Garstang area, coins of third and fourth century date were found.

The road from Ribchester to Kirkham and onwards to the coast seems to have yielded most in the way of chance discoveries, including coins of many periods. A hoard of denarii was found at Elston Hall; further along at Fulwood and Ribbleton coins of Nerva, Hadrian and Licinius (308–324 AD) are recorded, together with fourth and third century coins at Red Scar and in Haslam Park, both right on the road. Between Preston and Kirkham coins have come to light at Clifton (second century), and Treales (third century). Beyond Kirkham a first-century coin of Vespasian (69–79 AD) came from the Weeton area. W. Thornber, writing nearly 150 years ago, when the road was apparently much better preserved, lists a variety of artefacts found on or under its surface – horse-shoes, amulets, even a broken sword. It is impossible to assess, even approximately, the age or provenance of these finds, but it seems that they were remarkably plentiful (Thornber, 1851). Numerous discoveries have been made in the coastal area which was the probable destination of this road – three coins from Poulton, all early and including one of Claudius (41–54 AD); from Fleetwood two coins of Nero (54–68 AD) and one of Augustus (27 BC–14 AD), together with hoards of the first/second and of the fourth century.

There is in fact a wide distribution of find-spots of Roman coins in the Fylde area, even in places removed from Roman roads and settlements. This argues for a substantial population in the Fylde area in the Romano-British period (Shotter, 1990, 1995).

By contrast, surprisingly few finds, considering its importance, are known along the course of the road going eastwards from Ribchester to Elslack and, ultimately, York. A notable one, however, was the hoard of 1,000 denarii recorded by W. T. Watkin as having been unearthed by workmen in 1778 in the Middlewood area between Chatburn and Worston (Watkin, 1883).

Bibliography

Buxton K. and Howard-Davis C. L. E., 'Interim Report on excavations in the Ribchester Churchyard extension for Lancaster Archaeological unit', *Britannia* XX111, (1992) pp. 276–9.

Codrington T., *Roman Roads in Britain* (3rd edn, 1918), 104–5.

Edwards B. J. N., 'Lancashire Archaeological Notes, Prehistoric and Roman', *HSLC*, CXX1 (1969), p. 106.

Edwards B. J. N., 'Roman Finds from "Contrebis"', *CW²*, LXX1 (1971), pp. 27–33.

Ekwall E., *The Concise Oxford Dictionary of English Place-Names* (4th edn, Oxford, 1971).

France R. S., 'The Highway from Preston into the Fylde', *HSLC*, XL111 (1945), p. 27.

Harley, *Cartographical Notes; Reprint of the first edition of the Ordnance Survey of England and Wales – Lancaster and Blackpool* (Newton Abbot, 1970).

Jackson S., 'The Roman Road from Ribchester to Lancaster', *LCAS*, XV (1897), pp. 220–5.

Jones G. D. B., 'The Romans in the North-West', *Northern History* 111 (1968), 1–26.

Jones G. D. B., 'Roman Lancashire', *Arch. Journ.*, 127 (1970), 237–45.

Just J., 'The Seventh Iter of Richard of Cirencester', *HSLC*, 111 (1851), 3–10.

Leather G. M., *Roman Lancaster; Some Excavation Reports and some Observations* (Preston, 1972), RR/70D/1–7.

Margary I. D., *Roman Roads in Britain* (1st edn, 1957), pp. 104–109.

Ordnance Survey Map of Roman Britain; (4th edn, Southampton, 1991).

Shotter D. C. A., 'Roman Lancashire, Lectures to Eccles and District Historical Society', 3 (1973), p. 3.

Shotter D. C. A., *Roman Coins from North-West England* (Lancaster, 1990), pp. 220–33.

Shotter D. C. A., *Romans and Britons in North-West England* (Lancaster, 1993).

Shotter D. C. A., *Roman Coins from North-West England; First Supplement* (Lancaster, 1995), pp. 66–74.

Shotter D. C. A. and White A., *The Roman Fort and Town of Lancaster* (Lancaster, 1990).

Taylor H., 'The Ancient Crosses of Lancashire', *LCAS*, XX (1902), pp. 145–213.

Thornber W., 'Remarks on the evidences of Roman occupation in the Fylde district', *HSLC*, 111 (1851), pp. 57–67.

Watkin W. T., *Roman Lancashire* (Liverpool, 1883).

Occasional Papers from the Centre for North-West Regional Studies

Flowering Plants and Ferns of Cumbria	G. Halliday	£2.95
Early Lancaster Friends	M. Mullet	£2.95
North-West Theses and Dissertations, 1950–78	U. Lawler	£6.00
Lancaster: The Evolution of its Townscape to 1800	S. Penney	£2.95
Richard Marsden and the Preston Chartists, 1837–48	J. King	£2.95
The Grand Theatre, Lancaster	A. Betjemann	£2.95
Popular Leisure and the Music Hall in 19th-century Bolton	R. Poole	£2.95
The Diary of William Fisher of Barrow, 1811–59	W. Rollinson/B. Harrison	£2.95
Rural Life in South-West Lancashire, 1840–1914	A. Mutch	£3.95
Grand Fashionable Nights: Kendal Theatre, 1575–1985	M. Eddershaw	£3.95
The Roman Fort and Town of Lancaster	D. Shotter/A. White	£4.95
Windermere in the Nineteenth Century	O. M. Westall	£4.95
A Traditional Grocer: T. D. Smith's of Lancaster	M. Winstanley	£4.95
Reginald Farrer: Dalesman, Planthunter, Gardener	J. Illingworth/J. Routh	£4.95
Walking Roman Roads in Bowland	P. Graystone	£4.95
The Royal Albert: Chronicles of an Era	J. Alston	£4.95
From Lancaster to the Lakes – The Region in Literature	K. Hanley/A. Milbank	£5.95
The Buildings of Georgian Lancaster	A. White	£5.95
Lydia Becker and The Cause	A. Kelly	£5.95
Romans and Britons in North-West England	D. Shotter	£5.95
S. Martin's College, Lancaster, 1964–89	P. Gedge/L. Louden	£5.95
Walking Roman Roads in East Cumbria	P. Graystone	£5.95
The Northern Route Across the Northern Lake District	M. Allan	£5.95

Each of these titles may be ordered by post from:

> C.N.W.R.S.,
> Fylde College,
> University of Lancaster,
> Bailrigg, Lancaster

Books will be despatched post free to UK addresses.
Please make cheques payable to 'The University of Lancaster'.
Titles are also available from all good booksellers within the region.